Where Did They Get You?

Bridget P. McDonnell

TMP
Publications

First Published in 2013 by The Manuscript Publisher,
publishing solutions for the digital age -
www.TheManuscriptPublisher.com

ISBN: 978-0-9571157-4-3

A CIP Catalogue record for this book is available from
the British Library

Page layout, typesetting and cover design by
DocumentsandManuscripts.com

Printed and bound in Ireland

Where Did They Get You?

Contents

My Childhood

My life has had more twists and turns than a corkscrew, sometimes I made good decisions sometimes bad, luckily I survived them all and am still here to tell the tale. I was the second of seven children born in the 1940's on a farm in a very rural district in the west of Ireland. My sister Mandy was eleven months old when I was born, then two boys, Paschal and John which must have caused great excitement in such a male dominated society, and three more girls, Florence, Alma and Josie followed over a period of about 11 years. This was a small family compared to some who had anything up to twenty children, living on small farms or council houses with very little income. There was no birth control due to the influence of the Catholic Church, which had a very claustrophobic attitude to sex.

There was great poverty, particularly in the towns where people had to buy everything. There was no social security or benefits and many people had to emigrate. Some men had to emigrate and leave their families behind and only came home on holidays at Christmas. It was often said that some men had two families, one in Ireland and one in the UK. Education was not free and when children from large families came to 16 years they emigrated to the UK or to the US. Others went to work in shops or as domestic help and worked for their boards and lodgings just to "serve their time." Many Irish people had relatives in America who helped them out with jobs, usually labouring or domestic help and of course many became very successful; maybe not that generation but their children. It must have been devastating for parents to see their children emigrate to an uncertain future. I can imagine the homesickness must have been painful; there were no telephones and it would take a few weeks for a letter to arrive from America.

The expectation was that those who emigrated would also send back remittances to help out the families they had left behind. Families came to depend on such assistance in order to make ends meet. In fact the whole country came to rely on this system, in one way or another. Emigrant remittances constituted an important source of overseas earnings for a country like Ireland, helping the country through many rough patches and possibly keeping it afloat. For Ireland, emigration was a safety valve in more sense than one.

My parents were very lucky to have seven healthy children. Some parents lost babies at birth. The mother never saw and was given very little details of the baby. There were no bereavement therapies and women were not encouraged to express their feelings. They were simply told to get on with it: "that it was the will of God" and they could have more. I remember a family nearby had a cot death. I still remember the little white coffin leaving the house and everybody crying. Nowadays mothers can speak about such matters and have bereavement counselling, but then their grief was not acknowledged. There was a local family who were very poor. When the oldest son grew up he went to England to work on the buildings; he fell to his death. I remember the funeral passing my house when I was little, a memory which I will never forget. It was so sad to watch the mother as she walked out before the hearse. She had other children and they were very good to her, but I am sure she never recovered from the shock.

People who had land and grew their own vegetables were very kind and did give to the poor. A big family of itinerants lived in a tent locally and went from house to house to beg. They were never turned away without a pinch of sugar, flour, a drop of milk or potatoes. Their life span was much shorter than the settled community because of their poor living conditions.

We had a good-sized farm and we were self-sufficient. We had cattle, sheep, horses, pigs and donkeys. I loved animals and spent a lot of my childhood horse-riding bare back on a working horse. On reflection I was very brave and had no fear of anything. I was lucky never to have fallen off. I broke in a new donkey and taught him to jump a ditch. My father often said that I would be a famous horse rider one day. Sadly it did not happen. I was very hard working and was given a lot of responsibility at a very young age doing heavy manual farm work. We had three cows and my father assigned a cow each to my brothers and me. We were responsible for feeding and milking her. He told us that when the cow was sold that we would each get sixpence; not a bad deal for him as a cow was only sold every ten years. However it gave us great interest and responsibility. We were always very excited when the cow produced a calf.

My father always had workmen. Often it was people who came out from the orphanages looking for work. They worked for their keep and were often exploited; living in poor conditions and generally not treated very well. My father had farm machinery and a neighbour reminds me to this day of me, sitting on a hay turner pulled by a horse and my legs too short to reach the foot pedals. Nevertheless I did turn the field of hay. I also helped to prepare the soil for planting the crops with the horse and harrow. My father worked hard and was a good manager. He purchased a potato digger and teamed up with another farmer who had a tractor, which reduced the labour of digging potatoes with a spade. He was really forward thinking but sadly he got no support from my mother and nothing he ever did met with her approval.

He provided potatoes, vegetables, corn and all food stuffs to feed the animals and the family. He hand sheared 50-60 sheep and sold the wool. There was great demand for wool at that time and it generated a good income. We had apple trees, gooseberry and blackberry trees which were abundant with fruit in the summer months. We had many fun days going out to the fields picking mushrooms, putting salt on them and toasting them on the open fire. During the summer, when the lamb's tails were cut, we cleaned them and toasted them on the open fire - barbeques were never heard of then. The taste was juicy and succulent.

My father also cut turf, which provided fuel to heat the house and for cooking. Our summer holidays were spent on the bog and as a result I always had a great tan. When I went to town the other children remarked on it. I was embarrassed as I thought that I looked like an itinerant. We were self-sufficient and really needed very little cash. At Christmas we had turkeys and geese to sell, which bought all the winter clothes for the family. I remember cycling to town twelve miles away with my father before Christmas to sell turkeys at the market. He took me to a restaurant for dinner and it was rare to eat out in those days. At that time a restaurant was called an "eatin' house." We made butter, which took ages to make as we used a manual churn. Then my father purchased a milk separating machine which was less labour intensive and faster.

One of my many tasks was to go to the local the town on Saturday, to sell eggs and butter, which provided groceries for the week. If my mother gave me some pocket money I would be really chuffed. I remember digging the front garden to plant flowers; my father planted cabbage in it. This upset me greatly as I always had an altar to Our Lady in the house and needed flowers. I picked wild primroses instead. We had a big field of potatoes which we had to weed when we were on holidays. I remember standing at the end of the drills delighted that the job had come to an end and dying to get out playing. I said to my father that we had finished and he replied "start them all over again." There was not much leisure time in our house as there was always something to be done on the farm.

The economy in Ireland was poor and agriculture was the main industry in rural areas. Families who had farms could produce their own food, but people who lived in towns had to buy everything and it must have been very hard for them. Farmers were considered middle class people and the status was determined by the size of the farm. There was a church levy determined by the rateable valuable of property. The priest read out the names of the levy in order of their contribution, so everybody in the parish knew your status. Even though people were very poor they had to contribute, otherwise they were omitted off the list and were subject to ridicule and embarrassment. My mother would come home from Mass and say that such a family must have a very small "placeen" as they had contributed so little.

The priests lived in big houses and drove nice cars and the homilies usually included demands for money for themselves and the Missions. It was imperative to go to church every Sunday. At that time you had to be fasting from midnight before you received Holy Communion. One family would put on the pan at 11 pm the night before and eat a huge meal so that they would not be hungry next morning. Most people did not concentrate so much on the Mass as on other people; it was a hotbed for gossip and networking. Pregnancy would never be announced; the woman would start wearing the swagger coat. My mother would come home from Mass and say "there must be something doing" at this particular house. All issues to do with sex were undercover - metaphorically speaking.

My love for animals caused me great sadness, we had this donkey called Sam and I spent a lot of time working with her, bringing loads of turf from the bog and barrels of water during the summer when our local well went dry. It was a lot of responsibility for an eleven or twelve year old. The donkey did all the farm work and brought foodstuff from the mill to feed the livestock in the winter. She became old and we had trained her offspring. I was expecting her to have a leisurely life in retirement only to be told, when I came home from school, that she had been given to the itinerants. It brings tears to my eyes when I think of the unfairness of it.

Another memory was finding a stray puppy; somebody had dumped her from a car. I was pleading with my mother to keep her. Asking my mother for favours was not an easy task as the answer was usually "No." Dogs attacked sheep so we did not keep dogs. Eventually my mother gave in on condition that I pay the dog licence from my pocket money, which I was happy to do. The dog lived to a ripe old age and became a great family pet. When I returned home on holiday she was always excited to see me and remembered me.

Life was very simple and people had low expectations. There was great camaraderie and loyalty between the local people. The farmers got together to do the farm work in the harvest; this was called a "Mehill." There was very little machinery and work was labour intensive. The donkey and horse were essential to every farmer. There was no electricity or running water in the rural areas. We had to travel a few miles to collect water from a well. We made our entertainment by singing and dancing and staging our own variety shows. My father was a self-taught musician and local musicians gathered at our house. We had great music sessions. My father loved all kinds of music and could play many instruments by ear, which was an amazing skill. He went to the local opera every year. He always had the tin whistle in his pocket and would start up an impromptu session in pubs or any social gathering. He played anywhere and at any time and livened up a party with his lovely music. He played the flute as well as the tin whistle. He was taped by Ciarán Mac Mathúna at a famous session in the parish hall in the mid-1960's. His love of music brought him to many places and he was very well known. He travelled to county Kerry to take part in an All-Ireland Wren Boys competition in 1975. His gifted fingers brought countless hours of pleasure to many people over the years.

Looking back we should have been very proud of his talent; this was not so as my mother always led us to think that playing music was something cheap. Compliments were not in abundance from my mother. I can now only think that she was so jealous of his skills and the attention he got from people. He was a great wit and always told clever jokes. Years later, when my sister Florence was getting married, she hid his tin whistle so that he would not embarrass her at the wedding. On summers evening he played the tin whistle outside and people could hear the music for miles around. Neighbours talk lovingly about those times.

There was no traffic and the countryside was quiet and still. The sound of birds and bees was all that was heard. Travelling road shows came to the parish hall and my father would take us there. Rambling was a big part of village life and doors were never locked. The kitchen was usually very large and the main centre of the household. There was a big open fireplace with a big hearth. It was here that the family congregated around the fire to tell stories and discuss the day's activities. The neighbour or relation who visited was invited to come to the fire and there was a shifting of chairs to make the circle bigger.

Pranks were often played on other people for fun, sometimes with undesirable and unexpected consequences. There was a great sense of fun. My father told a story from a wake where a man who had a bad hump had to be tied down in the bed, somebody cut the rope and the corpse sprung up and everybody ran out screaming thinking that the man had come back to life.

My father had a very entrepreneurial mind and set up a country shop in the fifties. This was a great idea as there was no public transport and no big supermarkets. It was after the war and there was still rationing. My father had some contacts and got black market cigarettes. People came from miles around to buy them. There appears to be some stigma around doing this as people have often spoken negatively about it. This I could not understand as he was providing a service. It also meant that we got groceries at cost price. Most of the tea and sugar came in big bags and we had to weigh it out into smaller bags. Many small businesses started off in this way. My father appointed me to write letters to the suppliers. This sowed the seeds of entrepreneurialism in me as, in addition to my career, I always had some small business going. I was different from the other siblings and had different aspirations. It appears that I was like my father, which was probably the reason my mother treated me differently.

There was no public transport at the time and people walked or travelled by bicycle. Few people had cars. Farmers had to walk several miles with their livestock to a fair which was held on the street. If you did not go early you would not get a good position. I remember staying up until 3 am to see my father off to the fair. If the price was not right, the livestock would have to be walked home again. The fair day was a great event for farmers to meet, have a chat, a drink and often get a good bargain.

When I was about ten years old a neighbour taught me to knit and I knitted all the cardigans and jumpers for all the younger siblings. I was very compulsive and would stay up till all hours to finish a garment. Now many years later, when I look at old photographs I think of how clever I was to produce such work at such a young age. I remember finding some planks of wood in the barn and making a milking stool. I guess I was always looking for praise and approval from my mother but it never came. I always felt that I was being taken for granted. I remember going for days without eating to then make an apple tart and eat it until I was full. I did not realise the consequences of this on my metabolism at the time; just thought it was great to be able to go without food. I remember my mother shouting at me to eat my food, her tone of voice was enough to frighten me further.

I did not know anything about Anorexia Nervosa. It was the only power and control I had over my own life. I was also doing hard physical work and constantly knitting or engaged in some activity. I was very thin with very fine hair due to poor nutrition. When a young person cannot control anything else in their life, they can at least control their eating habits and weight. It has affected my life in so far as I have a constant obsession with dieting, exercising and weighing myself. I manage to cover it up well and do not make an issue of it. I use food for fuel not a recreational activity. I do have a small appetite and this gets commented on many times. The first thing I think of during festivities or celebrations is the fear of eating too much and being sick. I eat a very healthy diet and keep fit by swimming and exercising. I have gone on every diet you could possibly think of during my lifetime and am never happy with my body image; fortunately most people do not share my view, particularly the opposite sex. One thing I have in common with a turkey is that I am not too fond of Christmas.

Having the shop in our house was a great rendezvous and, on summer evenings, local children assembled there to play hurling and football. I got plenty attention from the local boys for my sense of fun and ability to compete with them at sports. We also learned to dance on the road and had lots of merriment.

My parents had a very turbulent relationship and the atmosphere was very unpleasant when they were there together. Lucky for him he was busy running the farm and only came into the house for meals. You would be forgiven for doubting that marriage was a "sacrament" if you lived in my house. My mother did not say too many complimentary things about my father and of course "mammy is always right" - we knew no better. We all grew up with the impression that my father was useless; which was far from the truth. We rarely engaged in any meaningful conversation with him for fear of meeting with her disapproval. The conflict upset me greatly and, on one occasion following a dispute with my mother I ran away to the fields. She and other siblings came looking for me. I was the subject of much teasing for ages. He provided well for nine people and we were never hungry or deprived. In fact talking to people later in life, they agreed that he was a very good provider. He loved children and did things to make us happy. He was always making fun. At Christmas he would set the alarm clock to ring and pretend it was Santa Claus taking orders for Christmas. Santa Claus usually brought clothing and bicycles, but no toys.

My father was an only child. His mother had been to America and there was a big trunk up in the attic with linen and other things she had brought back. She had a pair of ankle boots and gloves, which had money sewn into one of the fingers. I found this and it was so exciting. He was very conservative and held in high esteem by friends and neighbours.

My mother did all the cooking on the open fire. She was a very good cook and would make a big apple tart that was delicious. Americans were treated to this and said it was the best apple pie they had ever tasted. Considering they claim that they invented the apple pie this was a great compliment. She did not appear to appreciate how lucky she was to have children. Later in life I asked her "why did she have us?" She replied that was the way it was then. It appears that it was a match-made marriage. My father was very good looking eligible man with a good farm and quite charming; my mother came from a good sized farm and had a good dowry. She was also good looking and parishioners talked about how well they looked when they "shone out" at Sunday Mass following their wedding. Apparently he had been dating a local girl but rumour had it that my mother had a bigger dowry. I am sure my father regretted his decision. Dowries were essential. When a man married a woman who had inherited some land, he had to provide the dowry. One story is told of a man who was broke. He went to the bank and borrowed the money. By the time the wife found out where the money came from he had the ring on her finger and they paid the money back together. How romantic was that?

My mother's moods were very erratic. If we ever made a mistake or got into any trouble we would be terrified to tell her. If any of us got a slap at school we would tease each other that we were going to tell Mammy: so a lot of negotiation went on between the children. I remember on a windy day cycling my bike and was waving over and back up a hill. A car came and knocked me off the bike. The driver was an Englishman and he wanted to take me home by car. I declined the offer fearing what my mother would say to me in his presence.

She did work hard and we were always well turned out and greatly admired by neighbours, friends and teachers. There was a local dressmaker who made our winter coats which were always lovely and smart. We were well behaved, mannerly and got on well with everybody. Sadly our emotional needs were not met as my mother appeared to be devoid of any emotion: She was always abrupt, curt and cynical. Nobody knew what went on behind closed doors and we thought that it was the same in every home. She controlled her children with a mixture of emotional blackmail and guilt.

My older sister Mandy could do no wrong and had been given everything that she asked for. She was considered very bright and went to convent school by bus. Education was not free at the time and not everybody went to secondary school. There was a comprehensive school five miles away which both of us could have gone to as there would be no uniform costs or bus fares. My mother insisted that she wanted her to go to the convent, as it was considered better and more prestigious. Bus fares, school uniform and fees used up all the finances, which meant I could not go to school. Mandy also did some optional extras. She studied music and took dancing lessons and I learned from her. I asked my mother later in life why she spent all the money on Mandy and she explained that she was expecting that when she got a job she would educate the younger siblings. This was illogical as I was only eleven months younger.

I could not go to secondary school when I left primary due to financial restraints. My task was to work on the farm and help out with all farming duties. I was not at all happy having to stay at home but constant pleas to go to school went unheard. I was secretly planning to go and work in a shop just to get away from home. An auntie fell and broke her hip and I was sent to look after her. She lived with my uncle and 90 year old grandfather. I had to do all the housework and bring food into my grandfather in bed. I was terrified as I had never seen anyone so old. I would run into the room give him his food and run out again. I was scared to tell my mother or auntie of my fears and had to cover up and carry on as normal. I must have been there for about six weeks and then my mother sent for me. I presume my mother thought that I would inherit the farm, as did happen in those days when there were no offspring in the family. For my hard work I did not get one penny or any compensation. The only thing that I did get was plenty of praise and attention which I had not been accustomed to. I was only thirteen years old but very competent, reliable and responsible.

When I came home I was really pleased to see my other siblings. I was back to the grinding stone working on the farm, which I was not happy to do. I was becoming a young lady and wanted a more glamorous life, without having any idea what this was. I continually asked to go to school and had other members of the family pleading with my mother to allow me to go. Eventually she agreed and I went to the Vocational School (Tech) having been out of school for a year. A local girl was going from my area and we cycled 12 miles in all kinds of weather.

I had no difficulty settling into school and was doing well until another auntie was due to have a baby. My mother took me out of school to look after her children. So far I did not have much choice or respect in my life. I did return to school and resumed my studies, which I enjoyed. I learned to cook and made all the Christmas cakes and puddings for the family; prior to that the cakes were very basic. I made my own dresses and learned things with great ease. The technical school was for less academic pupils and there was some stigma attached to going there. The nuns in the convent would say to girls who were underperforming: "Oh there's no place only the Tech for you." The girls studied commercial subjects and domestic economy; the boys studied woodwork and metal work. One day Mandy was with the convent girls and I was with the tech girls. She did not acknowledge me and when I asked her about this she said that her friend did not like the tech girls.

A school friend was going away to work in a hotel for the summer months and I asked if I could go. Of course the answer was "No." I was told that I had to stay at home and work on the farm. My mother said that she did not wish her children to go out to work. Working on the farm was much more laborious with no personal financial gain. When I completed school I was just sixteen years old. I got temporary work in the County Council office for summer relief. It was wonderful having my own money. My mother expected me to give my cheque to her. Considering she did not want me to go to school in the first place I felt that this was unfair. I had very few material things and needed the money to get clothes for the dances. At that time only influential people got state jobs and you had to have "pull" so at the end of the holidays I had to leave.

I remember going to my first dance which was held to raise money for parochial funds. I had nothing suitable to wear and had to go to my cousins to get a blouse to match a skirt which I had made by hand. I was so shy I sat in behind the crowd; a neighbour spotted me and took me out to dance. My confidence improved as I went to more dances. Music and dancing became a favourite pastime. There were carnivals which were held in marquees. Back then most parishes built dance halls. We cycled long distances in bad weather to go dancing. Show bands were becoming very popular and provided great entertainment for rural areas. Neighbours who had cars would give us lifts. Getting permission to go was often a problem and we had to be on our best behaviour for a few days prior to an event. I always had a great sense of fashion and would often buy material and make my own clothes for a special occasion. I had a great sense of fun and learned to dance well. I soon attracted plenty of attention from boys. I remember my first kiss; a surge of emotion passed through my body. I guess it was the first love I had ever experienced. I finished school and got good marks in all my subjects. The only thing I lacked was confidence.

Shortly after I finished school I went to work in a local garage which was setting up. At that time there was no such thing as recruiting or advertising except for state jobs. Employers went to the Vocational School to seek out employees. This is how I was given the assignment. I had never used a phone and one day a call came for the boss. I put the receiver back and cut off the call. I had no idea how to set up accounts. It is easy in school under guidance but in reality I just had no idea about the general running of an office. This job terminated in an amicable way and I was recommended to another office. It was a plumber's merchants and I was expected, in addition to the office work, to go out to the yard to serve customers. This I refused to do. I was so unhappy and was unable to confide in anybody. There was no point in saying anything to my mother as she thought that money was everything and you should get on with it. I had no idea what I was going to do; I just lived from day to day and from dance to dance. My friend Margie was doing the entrance exam for psychiatric nursing and I decided to do it also.

We cycled fifteen miles to do the exam. My mother never expressed any interest in what I was doing. I had never thought of nursing but a sedentary life in an office did not suit me, having been accustomed to such an active life working on the farm. I was accepted and was overjoyed that there was a future for me; little did I know then what fantastic opportunities nursing would give me.

Leaving Home

I got the letter to go to the hospital which was 30 miles away, which at that time was a long way off. I informed my current employer and I was delighted to be leaving. They were pleased for me also. Packing was not a big issue, as I did not have much to pack, and I set off on my new adventure. I was sad to be leaving my siblings and I remember my mother saying that she would miss me for making the tea, one of the few compliments I ever received from her.

It was 1962 when I left home to commence my nursing career. I settled in very quickly. It was so exciting being with girls and boys of my own age, having my own room, access to transport and being away from my domineering mother. Living in the nurse's home was a lot of fun. We shared everything and doors were never locked. It was free from conflict; it had a real happy family atmosphere. When we were working meals were provided, but when we were off we got vouchers and provided our own food, which consisted of baked beans and bread. We had little cutlery and often resorted to drinking from jam jars. We did not have very high standards when it came to material things; money was put to better use to buy fashion and go dancing. Transportation was poor so needless to say I was unable go home very often. Secondly, when I did my mother was very demanding and expected me to provide money for the family. This upset me greatly as she was sending food parcels to my older sister who was working in Dublin.

Discipline was strict and we had to work twelve hour days with a few breaks. The work was not physically demanding: having to be on your feet was hard but nothing like the hard work on the farm. It was a very lively town and there was great activity around the hospital, which was the biggest employer in the area at the time. This was the early sixties and there was a great selection of showbands. We travelled for miles around the west of Ireland to dances. There was no problem getting a lift as somebody would always have a date, or else we hired a taxi. If we were working next day we had to be in at 11.30 pm; those rules were often broken. We were in bed and appeared to be asleep when the night sister checked in on us, then out the window before she got back to her office to resume dancing. Some very accommodating friend or date was waiting in a car to take us back to the dance. A date who was also a car owner was a great asset. We had to be sure that there was nobody lurking in the long grass to report us, but we were prepared to risk it.

My friend and I were almost sacked on one occasion. We were away on holiday and went back to meet some boys. When on holiday we were not allowed to stay in accommodation as we claimed living out allowance; so we sneaked in and slept in a friend's room. We were spotted and reported to the Night Sister by the Head Male Nurse. I was at home and received a letter to appear before the Residential Medical Officer. I made an excuse to my mother that I had to go back for a blood test. I got a local taxi to the train station but got there too late. The taxi man who was a neighbour took me there and did not charge me. I never prayed so hard in my life - my knees were red. My mother said that if I did not get what I was praying for there was no God. Discipline was so strict that people often got fired for less; but I must have displayed a great show of naivety and was acquitted. Matron wrote to my mother and luckily she did not say too much; only that jobs were difficult to get and that I would not get a good reference. I was so surprised at her reaction as this was one time I was not told off. This was the luckiest shave so far in my life;

one which could have changed my life forever. Once we were qualified there were no restrictions and we could stay out as late as we wished.

Some girls were going to the UK to do general nursing and I thought that I would also do the same; but I had been dating a very nice fellow, Sean, for some time and was not in any hurry to leave. I got a date to go to London but deferred it as I had not expected to be called so quickly. Sean went to work out of town and I continued to go dancing as, being very insecure I was afraid that he would find somebody else. He played football and was away for a game and not expected at this particular dance. I was seeing somebody else very casually and was out with him but I came back to meet my friends and nearly died when I saw him. I went over and I tried to cover up but he detected what was going on. A few days later I received a "Dear John" letter. I was really devastated but covered it up as much as possible; my pride would not allow me to admit that I had been dumped.

Emigrating

It was easy for Irish girls to get nursing jobs in the UK. Hospitals actually sent recruiting agents over to interview candidates. Another colleague of mine had gone to the same hospital and that was some help.

I made all the arrangements and travelled by plane for the first time. It was April 1967 when I left Ireland to further my studies in London. I arrived and made my way to the hospital alone. My friend was working but I guess she had given me some instructions. It was daunting not knowing many people and it did not hit me that I really had left Ireland. It was so different seeing all the different nationalities; there was only immigration and no migration. I had only ever seen a black person before on the cover of a Trocaire box. I was staring at a black bus conductor so much that he thought that I fancied him and he asked me out. I declined the offer and got off the bus and ran home swiftly. It was rare to see any black people in Ireland.

I was introduced to a few people. I remember going to see a movie with another girl. It was called *Some Like It Hot*. My friend was laughing but I could not muster a smile. She was giving me side glances and asked if I was enjoying it. I had to lie and say that I was. I have seen this movie many times since and can now appreciate how funny it is.

Soon after I arrived Sean wrote, informing me that he had decided to join the priesthood and that I would be welcome to come and visit him when I came home on holidays. He also said that he had been to London and even stood outside the hospital, but did not have the courage to come in. The seminary was not so far away from where I lived, but I could not entertain the idea of visiting as I felt it would be very strange to see him in religious garb, considering the fun we had shared for more than a year. He left the seminary after some time and got married and had a family.

I just got on with my restless life and did not have the courage to look him up again. There were many Irish girls at the hospital and there was great camaraderie amongst us. I settled in, made new friends and had to attend study for six weeks. I found it difficult to concentrate and was preoccupied with home. I was missing Ireland and my friends. It was not long however before my social life took off. I remember my first night going to the Galtymore club in Cricklewood, where most of the Irish people assembled. I was so devastated when I saw a sea of new faces and did not know anybody with whom I could dance with. Big Tom was on tour and playing *Gentle Mother*, which was a hit at the time. I was in tears. I thought to myself that this is a daunting situation. I am now a small fish in a big pond. Living in rural Ireland, there were not many places you could go that you would not know somebody

There were no time restrictions and we were out many nights until all hours, dancing and with our boyfriends. There were no dances allowed in Ireland during the season of Lent; so all the bands came over to the UK on tour. Massive crowds turned out. A dance hall owner in the west of Ireland held a dance during Lent, which met with the disapproval of the church. It was alleged that a girl was dancing with a fellow and when she looked down she noticed that he had hoofs. No prizes for guessing who was responsible for circulating that rumour. The priest thumped the pulpit on Sunday saying that it was the devil who danced the first step.

If we were not lucky enough to get a date with somebody who had a car, we hitchhiked and often got a lift home with the police. There was a police academy nearby and they would have known who we were. We thought this funny as in Ireland there was a great fear of authority and socialising with police was not usual. I guess it was at this time that I started to get more independent and realize that with or without my mother's criticism or approval, I was a very capable person.

We burned the candle at both ends and had great fun going around London on the tubes and buses visiting all the shops and boutiques. Fashion in Ireland was traditional: nobody wore miniskirts. My hemline was well below required standard and it took a bit of encouragement to change that. I got into the swing of fashion and then came the hot pants. I was denied admission to a Catholic club on the grounds that my dress was inappropriate, because I was wearing hot pants with bare midriff. I did negotiate with the doorman and was allowed in on condition that I wore a cardigan over the suit. Of course I had one wardrobe for London and one for Ireland, as dress was very conservative at home.

Student nurses were paid poorly, but bearing in mind that we were receiving a qualification, it was a good deal. Accommodation and food were deducted from our salary, so we did not have to go hungry. I really loved general nursing and it was much more interesting than I expected. I had enjoyed the study of psychiatry but practically, I did not find my role very fulfilling and was not really satisfied.

Ireland of 1940's 50's and 60's was a very intolerant place. Many of the patients had been put into care because they were rebellious, had had a child out of wedlock, or were responsible for some small misdemeanour. This resulted in many people becoming institutionalised when they did not require acute nursing care. There was one acute admission ward but only a very select staff worked there. The daily routine was the same. Also some of the staff had the same positions for years and were very set in their ways. They were strict and inflexible and promotion was by seniority. If one of the seniors took a dislike to you, they would give you a hard time and unnecessary duties.

There was a local shop who gave easy payment terms to nurses. We got some of our clothes there. We had to save to go home and got student reductions on flights. Many times we had to go home by boat as funds did not permit flying. The boats were very bad and I still remember people being sick all over the place. The boats have greatly improved since and are far more luxurious now. Money had to be put aside for social life, along with presents for all the family when we returned home. Most of the student nurses did extra work, either babysitting or working in nursing homes, which was extremely difficult in addition to full-time nursing. I found the study hard and sad to say, I failed my exams. I passed the practicals but academically I was a bit out of my depth. I was also distracted by late night dancing and boyfriends. I came home for all my holidays and was always pleased to see my friends and siblings. I would arrange my holidays to coincide with particular events, carnivals and cutting of the hay. I was always so sad leaving home, but could not show any emotion for fear of being jeered at. My mother never showed any emotion when I was leaving, which upset me greatly.

There was a big Irish population in London and throughout Britain due to the poor economy in Ireland. There was a great demand for labour to improve the infrastructure of the UK. My brother Paschal, who was heir to the farm also came over, a strange decision considering that my mother wanted me to stay at home and work on the farm. I met him at Euston Station. I will never forget seeing him standing there with his case. I knew he would have a hard time due to the fact that he had never been to a large city or away from home. He had no real skills and was ill-prepared for the fast pace of London.

My friend was over on holiday. We must have had a very late night and apparently we were late getting to the station. Many years later he reminded me of this. He omitted to thank me for meeting him, getting him sorted out with accommodation and keeping in touch to check on his welfare. The positive aspect of this story is that he met his wife through a connection of mine. He found it difficult to adjust to the pace of London for some time but he got married and settled down and they appeared to have a good life. It was sad to think that my father had paid labour most of his life and his son had now emigrated. When I came home on holidays most of my time was spent taking my father to get foodstuff for the animals or doing farm business.

A few years later my sister Florence and another brother John came over. I met them and helped them out until they got accommodation and employment. My sister was a hairdresser and had no difficulty getting work. I introduced John to a recruiting agency and he got working in a pub with live-in accommodation.

I had always lived in nurses' accommodation or a flat with automatic company laid on. Up to that time I had never given much thought to the loneliness, homesickness or isolation that other Irish emigrants experienced. People who had no connections were given some guidance by Irish Catholic organisations and given accommodation in hostels. It was no wonder that they had to resort to going to the pub and drinking to drown their sorrows.

I was becoming more cosmopolitan and broadening my horizons. Mixing with other nationalities made one more open-minded and free to express personal opinions and exchange ideas which would not be popular in a rural setting. Needless to say when I went home on holiday I had to be very selective and careful about voicing my opinions, particularly if it was anything to do with religion or sex. I remember expressing an opinion that priests should be allowed to marry. The reaction was one of shock and was not elaborated on further.

Many took advantage of the anonymity that London and other cities in the UK afforded them. They did not behave very well, resorted to alcohol to drown their sorrows and ended up in poor circumstances. There was enormous discrimination and often, when accommodation was advertised the sign said "no blacks, no Irish need apply". Others became very successful and now head some of the leading building firms in the UK.

Most of the labourers came from rural Ireland and were unprepared the fast life in the UK. Some men worked under different names and paid no tax. They had no GP and took great risks. If they had an accident they would have no insurance. I often encountered this situation when working in casualty. Many of the fellows were delighted to have an Irish nurse attending to them. A colleague once asked me why all the fellows were smiling when they came out following their injection. Men are not always the best patients and are squeamish about having injections. They would ask "is it going to hurt?" My reply was "the worst that can happen is that you could lose the leg." By the time they had digested this piece of useless information they would have their injection and would walk out smiling. A good sense of humour appears to be very therapeutic.

The political problems in Northern Ireland, which were at their height at that time, did not help matters and the English people were very suspicious of Irish people. In the UK there was always a great police presence outside the Irish dance halls, or any Irish venue at weekends, as there was usually a row fuelled by alcohol.

A large proportion of the nurses were Irish. Sometimes we got teased about our expressions and our religion. We went to mass every Sunday and obeyed all the religious obligations. The

English would always say "top of the morning to ya" and "begorra", which they thought was funny. I was late for work one day and apologised saying that "I had slept it out." The sister said: "You mean you overslept." We were very innocent, naïve and clean living. Some wore religious objects, which went down well with the older generation of Irish nurses who were in senior positions. The English did not appear to know the significance of those objects and made funny comments about the Church and the Catholic religion. We were too shy to deal with their teasing, consequently we stayed in our own Irish circles. Irish girls did not have a very liberal attitude to sex and did not take contraceptives, thinking that it was against their Catholic religion. Some were prepared to risk having sex without any precautions; which in retrospect was totally illogical. Irish girls were hard workers and well organised due to most of them having worked on farms; so they got on well with management and were greatly appreciated. Moreover we were well mannered and eager to please.

I passed my exams after a few attempts and with some difficulty. I was promoted to Sister at the age of 27. My friend and I were the youngest sisters in the hospital. We had difficulty fitting into the hierarchy of nursing, as most of the sisters were our superiors a short time before. We could hardly believe that we had been promoted at such an early age. We mixed with more junior staff; who we were more comfortable with. We relied on each other for support and to share the odd joke. One day my friend was having a discussion with a consultant. I got a pair of thick National Health glasses from one of the patients and stood discreetly behind the consultant as I was wearing them. Glasses in those days were not a fashion item. I can still remember the reaction on my friend's face. She had to excuse herself to get a patient's file.

I had a great fear of officialdom due to my childhood experiences. One day the matron sent for me and said that she had heard that I did not go to the sisters' dining room, I don't remember what I said but I never did go anyway. Another time I recall was when we had a big ball at Christmas, which all the senior management and administrative staff attended. I went along suitably attired with the boyfriend of the time. I felt very out of place and had a few stiff drinks just to give me some courage. A few days later there was a disco for the junior staff, which I attended dressed in hot pants and had a much more comfortable experience. A few days later matron sent for me to say that she had heard that I had been to a staff disco and that it was "conduct unbecoming" to a person in my position.

I really enjoyed my position and experienced great job satisfaction, as well as being appreciated by management, patients and colleagues. I was in a relationship which I was not happy with. It was my first intimate relationship and I found it difficult to sever ties for that reason. My strict Catholic views filled me with guilt and remorse. I thought that I would be turned away from the gates of heaven if I did not marry this man. This relationship was not without its difficulties; he wanted me to live with him with a view to settling down. It was Sixties London and most of the boys liked to play the field. I did not feel he was ready for commitment. I had some money saved in the building society for a rainy day. He got wind of this and asked me for a loan to buy a sports car. We signed an agreement and he agreed to pay me back monthly; which he did for a short period. When he got the car he was more interested in spending time with his friends and going to night clubs. Nevertheless he wanted to keep the relationship going. I got fed up of this and decided two can play this game - don't get mad, get even.

Being a dedicated follower of fashion I decided to update my wardrobe. The fashion was terrific; I bought a mini-skirt and semi-see-through blouse as well as white wet-look boots. I went to the Galtymore and really stood out because I was so trendy. I met a nice guy and he took me home by taxi. We were listening to music and chatting when I heard pebbles thrown at the window, then a knock on the door which I ignored. Next I heard some commotion in the kitchen and there he was having climbed up the pipes and in the back window. He was a fireman and this would not have been too difficult for him. He said to my date: "Hello mate, this is my bird and we have been going out for a long time." There were times when there was no man in my life, suddenly I had two: Happy days! He offered to drive the other guy home and, as there were only two seats in an MGB, I had to sit on the other fellow's knees, which was quite amusing.

I knew the only way to fully sever ties was to get away. That was when I started looking at advertisements in the nursing magazines. The government of Zambia was recruiting. I made an application and got invited for interview. I was accepted. At that time few people travelled, other than to the US and the UK. We were called the sunshine girls.

Most of my colleagues and friends had settled down and had families. I had a fear of commitment so I decided to move on. My relations thought that I was crazy going so far afield. Somebody asked me where was Zambia. I replied that it was in Africa, not realising that Africa was a very large continent.

I was living in a flat with three other girls. They wanted to further their studies and asked me to wait until they could leave too. This flat was a very noisy place: a radio blaring in one corner, TV in another, a record player on repeat with Big Tom singing country music. We had a mutual interest in country music; it was so sad and sentimental and we all grew up with it. When visitors came they would say 'which one are you listening to?' It was a bit difficult to answer this question. I suppose we were not listening to any one in particular, as it was our idea of background music.

There were plenty of boyfriends and there was never a dull moment. Fitting in work with social life was difficult. One day I was scheduled to work at 8am. I did not hear the alarm and did not wake up until 11.15 am. I jumped out of bed in a panic and ran to work, I did not even think of waiting for a bus. We had no phone in the flat. When I got to work I told the Sister that I overslept and offered to work my full hours. She was very sympathetic and said: "It's all right dear; most people would have called in sick."

I was not really convinced that my friends were serious about travelling, as they were always reminiscing about home. They also wanted to further their studies and we all hitchhiked to Liverpool for their interview to do Midwifery. I decided to go to Zambia on my own, knowing well that I would meet other nurses in the same predicament. We had a big farewell party which was enjoyed by all. When the time came to leave I was devastated and weeping; it had not really hit me until I had to say the final farewell. My friends were really shocked to see me so sad, as I had always been the life and soul of the flat.

Going To Africa

I went to Ireland awaiting my visa. My vision became impaired for some inexplicable reason, which caused me some anxiety. I had to seek medical advice. It must have been stress related as there was no physiological reason and it resolved itself soon afterwards. On the journey to Zambia we had a stopover in Nairobi and when the extreme heat hit me I nearly fainted: not surprisingly because I was wearing a long black maxi coat and had also had a glass of wine. It was the month of November 1971. I had never experienced such extreme heat as I had never been outside of Ireland and the UK.

We eventually arrived in the capital city of Lusaka, not knowing where we were going to be posted. It could have been anywhere in the bush, but luckily I was appointed to the University hospital in the city, which was very new and modern. My first impressions were a mixture of shock and surprise. I could not believe that anywhere could be so barren. My geographical knowledge was very limited. I had been brought up without television so my only picture of Africa was of the priests asking for money and pictures of children on a poor box. It was so hot and there was great poverty. People sat around under trees to get away from the heat. I found it amusing to see people using an umbrella to shield them from the intense heat, often riding a bicycle. There were plenty of other nurses from the UK and Ireland. We all got acquainted through our orientation programme.

The next thing to explore was the social scene. I was expecting that there would be discos and dances like London. I was surprised to hear that this was not so. I asked where you met people and was told people met at private parties and through acquaintances. There were plenty of private companies from all over the world working on different projects all over Zambia. There were copper mines in a town a few hundred miles away which offered contracts to overseas firms. It was not long before we got established and we had a "rare ould time." Julia, my friend from London came over but was sent to another area following orientation in the capital city. There was a party which we both attended. I was not happy with my date and told him that I wanted to go home. Julia borrowed a car and came and picked me up and we both returned to the party. His friends were there and obviously told him. Next day he came knocking on my door. I guessed that he was furious and did not answer the door. Julia was posted to the bush and got attacked by an elephant when out on a hunting trip with friends. Luckily she was rushed to hospital and made a good recovery.

Some people came because they were having marital or social difficulties - thinking that they would get sorted out but it did not always happen. The social life revolved around parties and being marinated in alcohol, which often clouded people's vision and exaggerated the difficulty. Working conditions were good and looking after the patients was rewarding as they were so grateful and easy to please. It was interesting to learn about tropical diseases and African customs. One day a man was behaving in a peculiar way and I thought that he was in pain, only to learn later that he was praying.

Relationships formed quickly and there was great camaraderie. Being away from families and familiar surroundings we depended on each other for friendship and support. There was no shortage of dates. There were plenty of social functions, some put on by different companies. There were always fellows looking for partners to attend. When I went on my first dinner date I was amazed at the silver service arrangement and thought;

what am I going to do with all the cutlery? There was no silver service in Burger King which was what I was accustomed to. I was still in contact with my fireman boyfriend and when I asked him for the money he owed me, he replied: "When you come back and get married you can have it," which did not happen. The sunshine was terrific and people looked so tanned. There was no talk of skin cancer at that time; it was a bit of competition to see who had the best tan. We would lie out in the hot sun for several hours, often getting third-degree burns. No wonder we were called the sunshine girls.

There were swimming pools, mostly at the hotels and it was a great rendezvous to meet talent. I was feeling out of my depth with all the highly educated, mostly professionals and often resorted to a drink or two or three to hide my insecurity. Fortunately I was always fairly well behaved, impulsive and funny, and friends were loyal and protective. I had a poor capacity for drink as I did not eat much; therefore I got drunk much faster than others. A neighbour from my childhood would say there was no blotting paper. One memory during my state of inebriation was that a fellow got sick and lost his false teeth. I went up to the band and got them to announce that a set of false teeth had been found; of course the fellow was too embarrassed to be identified. Being naïve and innocent does have its advantages at times, as he saw the funny side of what I did and did not say anything. I was often described as naughty-but-nice. Not being very cosmopolitan and having mixed mainly with Irish people where the conversation was usually parochial, I found it difficult to fit in. Irish people are said to be great conversationalists but out of their own circle of acquaintances, the content is not always of much outside interest.

People did a lot of reading and it was then that I developed an interest in books. I learned a lot about travel and improved my general knowledge, which had been sadly lacking. I was brought up without television or radio: the only newspaper we got was the local rag, which was full of gossip and local news.

There was a European drama group which put on plays and other entertainment for expatriates, some of whom had been there for many years. Movies were usually old by the time they got to Zambia. On days off there was no difficulty finding friends to travel around with. We had signed contracts for one year and if the contract was broken the employee would have to repay the airfare; which most people could not afford to do as the salary was very poor. Sometimes people would abscond across the border to Rhodesia (now known as Zimbabwe). Most of those areas were British colonies and many big engineering projects, such as Kariba Dam, had been carried out prior to Independence.

A colleague and I hitchhiked from Lusaka to Victoria Falls, one of the Seven Wonders of the World. It was very dangerous for girls to hitchhike in Africa but we had no sense of fear and took the chance. We were lucky and got there without difficulty. Sometimes other expatriates would have to come to the capital and they would be pleased to have company on the long journey back to their stations. There was a very strange custom, or so it was alleged, that if a foreigner was involved in an accident he would be held responsible and maybe put in prison.

Other trips were to Rhodesia for weekends, which was more westernised than Zambia. The country was named after Sir Cecil John Rhodes, the English-born South African businessman who founded the De Beers diamond company. Rhodesia is the colonial name that originally comprised both Zambia (Northern Rhodesia until independence in 1964) and Zimbabwe (Southern Rhodesia or simply Rhodesia after Zambia's independence). Europeans had settled and owned most of the land, which produced tobacco and fruit and other produce. It was one of the more prosperous of the African countries. It was more liberal for Europeans: western fashion and other commodities were available at reasonable prices. It was safer for women to go out unaccompanied as there was less crime in the cities. It bordered South Africa. With Independence looming however the white minority were opposed to the immediate introduction of majority rule, since this would have meant sharing of power with the black population. Their leader was Ian Smith, who was of Scottish origin. As Prime Minister he attempted to forestall the transfer of power with a Unilateral Declaration of Independence (UDI) in 1965. He failed to gain international recognition however. Independence and majority rule eventually came about in 1980, when the country became Zimbabwe.

The highlight of the year was going on safari to East Africa. Two friends and I flew to Nairobi. We met up with another girl and four of us booked the trip. It was the most exciting adventure I ever had. We had our own tour guide in a combo van and were able to drive right up beside the wild animals; we saw elephants, rhino, buffalo, gazelles, zebra and giraffe. We stayed in a wildlife lodge. We travelled to Serengeti Game Park and saw many more wild animals in their natural habitat. We even watched a lion killing a zebra, which was quite upsetting. We also witnessed a wildebeest and zebra being killed by a cheetah.

We travelled across to Tanzania; one waiter took us to see how he lived. He had a mud hut which was home to him and a few children. It was very well organized; just one big open space meticulously arranged. He was so proud of it. I was so moved I had to go out and cry. There was a display of dancing from a local nomadic tribe called the Masai, one of the many different tribes in East Africa. The Masai are a fierce fighting tribe of Bantu origin who live in Southern Kenya and Tanzania. They have their own culture and live by trading camels. They have their own dress code and were pleased to see western people. They were excited about having their photographs taken, and were not shy in requesting money for the privilege. A geologist took us on a tour of the Ngorongoro Crater and we saw a museum of ancient times and plenty more wildlife. We then travelled on to Lake Manyara to see the flamingos which were truly amazing, and we also saw pelicans sunbathing.

In addition to the wildlife, we met some two legged wildlife in the form of an Italian crew filming a programme for TV. Having been in the bush for some time they were hungry for female company. We had lots of fun, all very platonic, which was not exactly what they had in mind. One fellow offered to stay by my bedside in case wild animals broke into the lodge. I declined this offer and told him I was prepared to take the risk. Most of the lodges were managed and owned by British companies so they were all pleased to communicate with other Europeans. Most of the staff were local African people.

Next day we went to Ambossile National Park and Arusha and then back to Nairobi. It was a very enjoyable trip and we were exhausted, having had late nights and early mornings. We then flew to Mombassa and went for a swim in the Indian Ocean. Then on to Malandi with a plan to go snorkeling (or goggling as it is known there) but it was too windy. We then returned to Zambia and back to work.

Back at work I had difficulty settling. My freedom was compromised as it was not really safe for ladies to go out unaccompanied. I had a few months to complete on my contract and had made plans with another girl, Moira, to do some travelling in South Africa. I had applied to a hospital in Johannesburg and was accepted, but Moira was not successful. Soon afterwards I met a boyfriend, Thomas and this was a distraction for a while. As I had no intention of letting Moira down regarding travelling, I was torn. I finished my contract and went south to meet her. Thomas said that he would join us later. When I got there we did some sightseeing in Johannesburg and then went on to hitchhike to Cape Town, which was about 1000

34

miles away. We met very nice people who gave us lifts and often gave us accommodation and meals.

On one occasion the police asked us not to hitchhike on the motorway, but this did not deter us. We went to Table Mountain which Moira wanted to climb. This was a bit over-ambitious for me so we opted to go by cable car; the view was amazing. We went to see diamond mines and wine distilleries and really enjoyed the beautiful scenery and hospitality of the people. Nelson Mandela was in prison in Robben Island at this time, which we could see from afar. We hitchhiked back to Johannesburg and stopped off at various places on the way. We had been staying at the YWCA which was cheap and cheerful. The management were white but most of the staff were African. We were wearing low cut summer dresses to suit the hot climate and were told that this was inappropriate as it offended the male staff. Thomas arrived and I joined him at his hotel, also reserving my bed at the YWCA. Next morning we met Moira with our entire luggage telling us that we had been evicted from the hostel.

We decided then that as we did not like the big city, which was so noisy and busy, we would go to a smaller place and chose Durban which is a seaside town. Moira got a job in a local hospital and I went travelling with Thomas. We went on an overnight train to Cape Town. It was a pretty unimpressive mode of transport as the weather was so hot and air-conditioning was poor. He informed me that he had been offered a very lucrative contract in Zambia and asked me to go back. I did not want to return as I knew that I would not be happy to stay there any longer. Also I did not want to let Moira down. He returned to Glasgow for family reasons and I joined Moira in Durban.

One bank holiday weekend we were going to Mozambique for the New Year celebrations. We planned to hitchhike but the cars were all full and nobody stopped to pick us up. We were on the road for hours in the soaring heat. A long distance lorry driver, who was Indian, stopped and in we jumped without hesitation. It was the height of apartheid and we were so fed up we accepted and were willing to live dangerously for a while. The consequences were not something that that we had given much thought to; the excitement was thrilling. If we saw police we would hide, as mixing with coloured people was an offence punishable with a prison sentence.

After this we decided to buy a car to travel around and found a Volkswagen Beetle which was in good condition. We had many exciting and narrow escapes in this car. Moira had a full driving licence but I did not. I eventually did my driving test and was lucky to pass. One time we went to a game park where animals were living at large. We saw a lovely lake and decided to have a break to view the beautiful scenery. When we decided to leave we discovered that we were stuck, not a soul to be seen. There were signs all over saying: "Please do not alight from your vehicle, wild animals roaming freely." We were worried and amused in equal measure and frequently got out of the car to see if we could attract some human attention. Eventually park keepers came and spotted us. They got several African men to pull us out manually, shouting "heave-ho, heave-ho" in unison as we got extricated from the mud. Another lucky escape!

We had many more enjoyable trips around South Africa. We worked for a few months to save some money and were there over the Christmas period. We were assigned night duties and, being desperate to top up the funds, we did not have much choice. It was a bit lonely coming off night duty on Christmas morning, sitting out in the garden drinking brandy to celebrate. It may sound exciting but it was one way of drowning our sorrows at such a family time. My father often said that it would be great to have Christmas in the middle of summer; I didn't think so on that occasion. It was a Jewish hospital and Christmas celebrations were low key for the gentiles, with a very mediocre dinner.

We worked there for a few months and then decided to go to Zimbabwe to make visits with Thomas more accessible. We were due holidays for the period we had worked, which were denied, and we were not given any pay or time off in lieu. We were not too happy as we should have been paid for one week's holiday. Moira was off on the final night, which was when we got paid. I presented for work in uniform, collected my cheque and out the back door. I imagine it was not the first time this had happened and that was the reason why we were not paid until we presented for duty on the final night. We were in contact with some colleagues and they told us that there was great commotion finding cover at short notice. The car had some difficulty starting at times and Moira parked on a hill to ensure we got off hastily without a hitch. The hasty escape from Durban was very exciting as we took off at such speed.

Moira befriended an Australian girl, Cheryl, who requested to travel with us. We had a leisurely trip via Pretoria, stopping off to see vineyards and local attractions, and then on to Bulawayo. We decided to travel on to Salisbury, now known as Harare, which was the nearest point to Lusaka in Zambia. Taking another traveller on board did not turn out to be such a good arrangement. Cheryl had run out of funds and borrowed money from me to get her ticket to travel to London. She promised to repay me when she got to London. I did not hear from her and had no address to contact her; no hope of getting my money back. Moira and I went to hospitals in the capital city of Harare looking for work. The matron at the hospital was a very casual person and said: "I will take you because I need a Psychiatric Sister to act while the regular Sister is on extended leave in Italy." Moira had to go to a hospital in a rural area sixty miles away and was employed as a midwife. At first we were both delighted; we agreed to share the car, one week each. I really loved my position and got on well. It was a very challenging role in charge of a 30-bedded mixed psychiatric ward with an all-female staff.

The professor was Scottish and did not like the regular sister. Being Irish we got on well. The Mental Health Act was strict: the court had to be notified of all patients who were detained so a lot of paperwork was involved. I had great support from my colleagues as they had been there for some time and knew the ropes but did not have the appropriate qualifications. Even though there was no official apartheid in Rhodesia there were separate hospitals for the caucasian population. At that time Zimbabwe was the garden of Africa and was very prosperous and self-sufficient. Even though it was land-locked it had good relationships with the UK and South Africa. Most of their trading was conducted with both of those countries. There were big tobacco farms which were run by white farmers and labour was provided by the indigenous people.

I was very happy when at my work. I visited Moira, who appeared to settle in well to the rural area as it was easier to make friends. Thomas also visited some weekends. It was so difficult to make friends as most of the staff were settled families with their own responsibilities and social scene. I did not have much in common with them. They were quite parochial and had not much interest in anything outside their own social circle; many had never travelled outside of their own small environment. They did everything to make me feel welcome and were very supportive at work, but I felt so lonely at times when I was not at work. I completed my contract and decided to return back to the UK. I informed Thomas and he also decided to return to the UK in November 1973.

We did a stopover in Rome and visited the Vatican City where we climbed to the top of the Sistine Chapel, which is quite an achievement, then to the Coliseum which is one of the most visited monuments in the world. We visited several museums and other sights of interest and I threw my coin in the Trevi fountain.

We then went on to Egypt and spent some time in Cairo, Africa's biggest city. It was such a busy noisy city with people driving around blowing their car horns as the driving was so erratic. There are a maze of Souks/Markets with a variety of different crafts and jewellery. Then to the Museum of Antiquities, the home of many treasures recovered from the Pyramids; and at last to see the Pyramids at Giza. We went for a cruise on the river Nile, the longest river in the world. The cruise was from Aswan to Luxor and included the riverside temples and sights of interest.

We then went to Cyprus and spent a few days there to relax. At that time Cyprus was divided politically between Turkey and Greece. There was political unrest and the army were present on the streets. We proceeded to go to Paris and saw the sights there. We climbed to the top of the Eiffel Tower. When we returned to the UK it was November and I will never forget how nice it was to see rain and experience some moderate climate. I never realised how much I had missed the seasons as sunshine every day can be very boring.

I went to Ireland to visit my family and Thomas came to visit me later. He was a Scottish Protestant and I did not take him to meet my mother, as I was afraid that she would not approve. I decided to join Thomas in Glasgow. Initially I felt homesick from leaving home again. I joined a nursing agency and was soon working in a local hospital.

Some people were very friendly but there was a very anti-Irish feeling on account of 'the troubles'. At times I was afraid to speak and let people know that I was Irish on account of the anti-Irish sentiment. My colleagues were friendly and as I was living in the nurse's home it was easy to make friends. One day at work we were in the staff room watching *Top of the Pops*. The Ian Dury song, *Hit Me with your Rhythm Stick* was being performed. Some of the doctors started singing "Hit me with your shovel Mick." I was so humiliated and embarrassed but could not show it. I was the only Irish person present and was not amused.

There was also great rivalry between football teams and the anti-Catholic sentiment was very obvious. I was working with a doctor one day doing a procedure and all the time he was insulting me and saying that I should be ashamed of the behaviour of the IRA. I guess he was expecting a reaction but at that time I was defenceless due to my lack of knowledge about the situation. I regret to this day that I did not walk off but that might have had professional consequences.

I felt that my education was sadly lacking and I started reading: mainly books written by Patrick McGill which included *The Rat Pit, Children of a Dead End* and *Moleskin Joe*. Those books were about the many Irish emigrants who went to Scotland to pick potatoes. Those people had dreadful lives and I had not known anything about it. They were resilient and resourceful and survived terrible situations. They were never negative and lived from day to day and were very supportive to each other. They were hopeful for a better future. Some of the books I read were autobiographical and it was difficult to believe how people survived their dreadful experiences. One author wrote an article for a paper and subsequently got a job as a journalist in London. He did not fit to this scene as he was out of his comfort zone and returned to Scotland as a navvy. He had missed the camaraderie and freedom of travelling around and keeping in touch with his colleagues.

I enjoyed working in Glasgow and made good friends at work. Some of the girls were going to America and as I always had a desire to go there, I decided to go also. I did not feel comfortable living in Glasgow. As a Catholic and Irish I felt insecure and resented. I did not feel that the relationship with Thomas would work due to the fact that he was not Irish or Catholic. I also got vibes that his family were not in favour of what they called "a mixed marriage." His family lived in a posh part of Glasgow. His father had just died and his mother lived alone. I stayed there until I got a job and then moved into nurses' accommodation. I often felt uncomfortable in non-Catholic circles as there were always some uncomplimentary comments about religion and Irishness. I was reminded many times of the famine. I was also fearful of commitment due to my previous problems with relationships. I made up my mind to go to America and informed Thomas of my decision; of course he was disappointed.

Going to the USA

I applied for my visa and was accepted for the position of staff nurse in a private hospital in Fort Worth Texas in April 1974. The excitement of going somewhere new was great. I was beginning to see that for me, excitement is one of the necessities of life. I hanker after it like a hungry man for food. Rather than dealing with issues I just ran away. I set off and, as we know, everything is bigger and better in Texas.

Having grown up in rural Ireland with no cinema, I was not too familiar with Western movies, which surprised most of the locals. The big shopping malls were amazing; people were eating out in restaurants, which was not usual in Ireland. Everybody lived in the fast lane and drove around in big cars. Working conditions were great and the status of a nurse was very good. There was a housekeeping department which did the entire domestic and cleaning work. There were nursing assistants to do the more menial tasks, the system was so different and better organised than in the UK. There was a public health system which was for the less affluent population. Most people had private health insurance which was very efficient.

We had a period of orientation to learn Americanisms. The salaries were good but annual leave was two weeks per annum compared to six weeks in the UK. If we wanted to go on a trip home we would have to take unpaid leave. The hospital was staffed by many overseas girls from the UK and Ireland so it was easy to make friends. The Americans were very excited to hear our accents and would ask us to talk. Of course many had an Irish heritage; it didn't matter how long back it was they were still

Irish. Of all the overseas girls the Irish were the most popular and well respected. Some of the British girls told Americans that to them the Irish were what like Mexicans were to the Americans; which was not very complimentary.

I had a friend living in Corpus Christie and decided to go and visit her. Corpus Christie is on the Mexican border and we travelled to El Paso and Monterrey, which was an eye opening experience. As we had not been paid I had $50 in my pocket, but met some very accommodating person who lent me money until I got paid. I had to resort to going on the greyhound bus which took twelve hours to get there, an exhausting but exciting experience. Only poor people or tourists used the bus service. I had never lived on credit but decided to get a new car just to keep up with the Jones's. I had to do my driving test which was not too difficult. The motorways were truly daunting and it took some time to adjust to driving on the right side. I had very little driving experience and it was a difficult task driving into the multi-story parking lots. I had a few lucky escapes, my friend Mary and I drove to Corpus Christie to see my friend. I was taking instructions from a backseat driver, at a big junction he told me to drive on; unfortunately I did not realize that he meant when the coast was clear. A car came at great speed and hit the front of my car and fled the scene. I had to drive back to Fort Worth with a very bashed front.

Another day I was driving into a car park, the barrier came down and hit the front. My insurance company were not too pleased and would not renew my insurance. There was an insurance company who took on high risk drivers and I had to be taken on by them. Eventually after some experience my confidence grew and I became a very good driver.

There was always the opportunity to do overtime, which was necessary to pay the bills. The letters also came from home to get different toys which were not available in Ireland. I derived great pleasure from giving and making children happy. Having the latest toys made them so. Most of my friends worked from 3pm to 11pm and the social life took off. We were all a great novelty to the American men and had lots of fun. We would go out and come home rather inebriated, having been treated to free drinks from our male admirers. We often went to work at 3pm nursing a bad hangover. After a bit of hydration and some food we were ready for the road again after work. Being country girls we were brought up listening to country music, so the Irish girls were in their element.

There was a big Country and Western venue called Stage Coach which all the cowboys frequented. It was not hip to be a Country and Western lover so we had to conceal the fact that we frequented those venues to our American work colleagues. There was often a shootout and locals thought it was unsafe. The cowboys drove pickup trucks and ours were the only cars outside the venue. The cowboys were fascinated with us and some of them would be proud to have Irish heritage. There was no shortage of escorts to take us to see rodeos and to show us around Fort Worth. They thought that we all learned English since we came and had only spoken Gaelic in Ireland; and of course they had all heard about leprechauns. Their knowledge of the world was very limited. They were very polite and would remove their Stetsons, leave them on the table and say "would you like to dance maam." The sunshine was great and most of the apartments had swimming pools. Often on our way home from the night clubs we would go swimming or to an all-night restaurant for breakfast.

There were plenty of concerts and as there was a big conference centre in Fort Worth; most of the big groups came on tour. The Rolling Stones featured with The Eagles as opening act. Mick Jagger strode on to the stage wearing a purple cloak, which he divested himself of prior to performing. As the locals say "it shure as hell set my hormones a-churning." We also saw Led Zeppelin, Elton John, The Who and many more famous acts. The most exciting concert was Elvis Presley. Wendy, my friend said that she never saw his face, meaning that she was focusing on his gyrating hips and his skin tight jeans. There were many Country and Western acts and Willie Nelson was just becoming famous. I also saw Cat Stevens, whose music I had always loved and enjoyed. I later met him in person in London, in the course of my nursing duties and got a tape from him.

Theatre was a rarity but sometimes there were good productions. One was Cid Chereese in a famous play, *Move Over Mrs Marcum*. A production of the Opera *Carmen* also came, which the Americans were all talking about. Just to fit in, my friend and I went but slipped away surreptitiously at the interval. At that time Opera was not on our curriculum. The atmosphere was very different to what I had been used to. Americans thought that there was no place like their country and everything was bigger and better. They were very materialistic and their ambitions were to be millionaires; those ambitions I had never even thought about.

I had applied for my permanent visa and was unable to leave the country; otherwise I would have to go back to the bottom of the queue. As a result, most of the annual leave was spent on trips around America. We travelled around Texas. Dallas was quite near Fort Worth and we saw where President Kennedy was assassinated. The ranches were vast, consisting of several thousand acres. We also saw The Alamo, where many battles were fought and many more movies were made about it. It has great historical significance in the southern American states. There was a hit record called *Show Me the Way to Amarillo*. We went there but it was just a wild Texas town. We travelled to Nashville, Tennessee to see the Grand Ole Opry House and then on to New Mexico to see all the Indian Reservations, which were quite fascinating.

There are twenty-two Native Indian Tribes. The rich and vibrant Native American history is celebrated in museums, ceremonial dances, arts, crafts, language, villages and lifestyle of New Mexico's tribes. Approximately 1500 years ago, Ancestral Indians living as hunter-gatherers throughout the southwest, joined together to establish permanent settlements known as Pueblos. Other groups such as Navajo and Apache continued their nommadic lifestyles. For some New Mexican tribes this way of life continued into the 21st century. New Mexico tribes have witnessed and experienced many changes in their long histories. The development of modern casinos, resorts, hotels and golf courses for their visitors have greatly improved their economic status. They also produce beautiful hand made jewellery arts and crafts. They are very friendly, easygoing people, eager to talk about their lifestyle and love to perform their ceremonial dances. Their costumes are quite elaborate and colourful.

In New Orleans we drove around Bourbon Street, to look for accommodation which would be convenient for the night life. We saw a sign and, as it was difficult to park, my friend went in to book. She came out looking worried and said: "I have booked but it is not very nice." I went in and was shocked; there were weird men standing at the bar, there was a half door to the bedroom. There were crumbs in the bed and the bed linen was not too clean. I quickly deduced that this was not the place for us as it appeared to be a brothel. I asked the male receptionist if we could have our money back as we were not happy with the place. Initially he was reluctant and said that his boss would "chew his cock off" if he refunded the money. After some persuasion and giving the excuse that we could not get parking, he did give us a refund. It was an eye opening experience.

We got other accommodation and enjoyed soaking up the atmosphere in the French Quarter. The French Quarter is the original 18th century French settlement and is in the heart of New Orleans. New Orleans is 70 degrees below sea level and is prone to very severe hurricanes because of its location in the Gulf of Mexico. It has a unique mix of African, European and Creole traditions. It hosts many street festivals and parades with good and ever present jazz music. New Orleans is the birth place of jazz and one of the best places in the world to hear good jazz. The St Charles streetcar, which dates from 1835, clanks its way around the city. The Warehouse district has a cluster of big hitting museums; including the Civil War museum, which is a relic from the Deep South, looking back to the 'Lost Cause' of the Southern Confederates.

We travelled to the Deep South and saw some of the plantation houses which I had read about in the novel, *Gone With the Wind*. It was not all rich as portrayed on TV; there were very underprivileged people living in rural areas of the Deep South. It was very religious and there were dry areas where no alcohol was available. We saw segregation in some areas. Another trip was to San Francisco where we visited all the sights and travelled on the trams. We went to Universal Studios and were fascinated at how the stunts were done. During this trip Mary decided we would go for a pre-dinner drink; we went to the first Irish pub we could find. A crowd of Irish fellows from a building site came in and when they heard our accents they showered us with drinks. I always had a poor tolerance for drink and, not having eaten, I was drunk in no time. Mary was not too happy as, when I sobered up I could not look at another drink.

On another trip to Las Vegas we went to some concerts at Caesars Palace. There was an entertainers strike going on and we got in free to see Petula Clarke and other acts. Nobody asked us for money. We hired out a car to see the Grand Canyon and drove all over Colorado.

I went on a planned trip to Mexico; alone as none of my friends were available. I met up with another girl in Mexico City, who was also travelling by herself. It was a beautiful city full of culture, colourful markets, brilliant architecture and many interesting museums. We travelled to Acapulco, stopping off on the way to see a silver mining town. The beach was very pleasant but there were so many hawkers we did not feel safe. Poverty was very obvious and there was a lot of begging. I was afraid of being robbed but kept to the good districts and had no problem. As Mexico shared a border with Texas there was much illegal immigration. Many lost their lives attempting to gain entry to the US by swimming across the Gulf of Mexico, hoping for a better life. There was very strict border control both day and night. I got the feeling that Mexico was a mixture of Ireland and Africa.

There was a long waiting list for permanent visas and I was beginning to get home sick. I suppose the fact that I could not go was making it more difficult. I was getting a bit claustrophobic. I remember going to a movie called *Barry Lyndon*, a story of an Irish emigrant and I cried all the way through. Eventually I got the visa and planned a trip home.

On my first visit home after two years, I recall embracing my mother, the only physical expression of affection I had with her, which was initiated by me. I was so pleased to be home, I hired a car and my sister Alma and friend Maura did a tour around Ireland; which included a trip to Bunratty Castle and to a medieval dinner. I really enjoyed the trip, driving through the beautiful countryside, listening to music and having fun with the locals. The beautiful green fields were a great contrast to the barren countryside of Texas. It was then that I began to realise that I did not like the fast pace of America and never really settled when I went back.

The job situation in the UK was not very good. So the only way to have something to return to was to do further study. I applied for different courses and was accepted for one in London. Like all my other experiences I was really sad leaving my friends; they could not understand why I was leaving if I was so sad. Probably the main reason was that I had no love in my life; material things were not enough. I always felt lonely. I did not fit in with the American social scene as there was a lot of promiscuity, which I did not want to be part of. My relationships were always meaningful and casual sex did not interest me, which was probably due to my strict Catholic upbringing. My heart always ruled my head when it comes to love; I was afraid of falling in love and having to spend my life in America. Some of the girls had married Americans and when others were going home, they often regretted that they could not go also. I also had a genetic pull towards my homeland, but employment prospects were poor in Ireland, so I hit for London.

At this time I was very unsure of myself. One fellow asked me why I was so insecure since I appeared to have everything: good looks, good personality. At the time I could not answer this. I have always been told that I was a Shirley MacLaine look-a-like. I went into a store one day and the assistant asked me what my name was. Of course I thought that I had done something wrong. I asked why she wanted to know. She replied that she thought that I was Shirley MacLaine. In fact I was told that when I was a student nurse in London, but at that time I did not know who she was. I drank more than I should just to cover up my insecurities and was lucky that I did not have an accident. Once I went to a friend out of town for dinner. When I was coming home, rather inebriated, I ended up on the wrong side of a slip road going on to a motorway. It is hard to believe but, at that time, there was no issue about drinking and driving and everybody did it. The police noticed me and put me on the right track, one of my many lucky escapes.

On my trip home I stopped off in New York and booked some tours to see all the amazing sights. It was so easy to get around New York as the maps are very clearly presented. I was fascinated at the size and designs of the buildings. It was not safe for a female to walk on the streets unaccompanied in Texas; a friend of mine had got mugged previously, which made me more cautious. So the sense of freedom in in New York was amazing. It was safe to walk and go shopping there. I contacted an old friend from the past who lived in New York. Some Irish people think that the only sights worth seeing are pubs; so I was taken on a tour of the Irish pubs. I was staying in a hotel on Broadway and went to see *Hair*, which was very controversial at the time; I was not expecting to see nudity on stage.

Back In London

I arrived in London to take up my new position as a staff nurse in April 1977. It was difficult to get nursing positions at that time so I decided to do some post graduate training in Renal Medicine. As always life was so exciting and I was glad to be back on familiar territory. I was allocated accommodation and was shocked at the size of my room. I had been living in a big apartment in Texas with all mods and cons overlooking a swimming pool. It was a room subdivided and would not be adequate to even unpack as I had all my earthly possessions with me. I pointed this out to the warden and was told there was nothing better available at that time but that I could have the next available one. Lucky enough a bigger room came up soon after. There was a mixed group of other employees in the accommodation. We had a fairly good social life and the novelty was great for a while. There was always somebody to go out with. We went to the theatre in the West End, which I was developing a taste for, or else we went dancing to Leicester Square. There was one fellow in the group who was trying to impress me with his dancing. He was doing the splits and his trousers ripped; this caused some amusement.

One day I walked into the dining hall and who should be sitting there but Cheryl, the Australian girl who I had lent money to in Zimbabwe. I went over to her. She said: "I don't think I know you." I reminded her and she blushed. She arranged to meet me again but that never happened, neither did I ever get my money.

I was not happy with the nursing course that I was doing and when I got my first pay cheque I just could not believe it: the salary was so poor compared to USA. I had a friend working in a private clinic which offered better salary and accommodation. I applied there and was accepted. I looked after many celebrities and it was a novelty for a while. It was exciting as we never knew who was coming in. Having only seen those people on TV or the stage, it was amazing to be actually talking to them. There were many other nationalities, mainly from the Middle East, which made the role more interesting. I was able to learn a few words of Arabic and to interact with other cultures. The role of a nurse in the private sector was disappointing. Nurses had to do a lot of non-nursing duties, which would have been done by nursing assistants in the public sector. I was not too happy with that aspect of my career. It meant less time spent dealing with the psychological and medical needs of the patients. I plodded along and tried to make the best of it.

The entertainment in London was terrific and there was always some place to go. A few friends were going to Irish dances and I was excited about going, only to discover that nothing had changed. They all appeared set in their own world and reminisced about home; many stuck in a time warp. There was a lot of drinking and their behaviour was something less than acceptable. I had grown apart from this way of life and found it quite boring. My views were more cosmopolitan and out of touch with their little world. Soon I began to miss the glamour and glitz of America. I missed all the attention from the opposite sex. In America most of the parties were held by someone we knew so it made it easier to socialise and establish contacts. There, the overseas girls were in great demand and a novelty. In London it was more difficult to get into a social circle with interesting people, as nursing is mainly female dominated. I had been living in a rather luxurious apartment and now, living in one room with plenty of restrictions did not help matters.

I spent time with friends and had the occasional boyfriend but was not really happy with my life. I immersed myself in cultural activities and spent time sightseeing, going to the theatre and museums, which I enjoyed. One of my first Irish plays to see was *The Plough and the Stars* by Sean O'Casey, which was very enjoyable. I was developing a great interest in the theatre, something which I had not explored previously. I was not happy but always kept the bright side up.

I mustered up a bit of enthusiasm and started to do some travelling. A friend and I decided to go to Greece. We looked up brochures and thought that it would be good to go overland as finances were low. There was a trip advertised from London to Athens in a luxury coach which just suited our budget. We lived in the Regents Park area, which is near Camden Town, from where the trip started. We went along and when we got there we were told that the luxury coach was not available. Another one was put on which was far from luxurious. Some Greek people were returning home and we set off with a load of cargo, including mattresses and all kinds of everything on the roof. We were so amused, as we looked like a crowd of refugees being evacuated from some war torn part of Africa. Nevertheless we saw the funny side of it and thought it part of the adventure. An overnight break in Austria brought some relief. There were some amusing characters on board and we had a good laugh; it was not all negative. The suspension on the bus was not too good; travelling on the bad roads through Yugoslavia was a jaw rattling experience. By the time we arrived in Athens we were ready to book into a physiotherapy department. After a full night's sleep however, we made a good recovery and started to enjoy the holiday.

Island hopping was a great source of amusement and we had a good time meeting the local people. We spent some time in small villages where we were a great source of excitement. Two other friends went on a package holiday and we met up with them. I was glad that we had gone freelance as the tourist areas were very commercialised, catering mainly to the holiday-makers. Most of my holidays were adventure/culture trips, which meant that we moved to different areas. Many tourists did not explore much of the islands. They enjoyed the drinking and discos and did the usual tourist trips. There were plenty of predatory Greek men; the story of Shirley Valentine rings a bell and was really true to life. We were not short of Greek attention, as local women do not go out unaccompanied and are quite religious and traditional. Arranged marriages are still common; they prefer to marry within their own culture and station. We returned to London with a great story to tell and very pleasant memories.

That kept me happy for a while and soon after I met a boyfriend. His name was Geoffrey. He was from Somerset and he had an MGB sports car. We spent many good holidays touring Devon, Cornwall and Somerset in the summer months. He enjoyed theatre and sports and we enjoyed some good times together. But it was not a relationship which would have worked. He was anxious to come to Ireland; but at that time being Irish was not fashionable due to the problems in Northern Ireland. Being a nurse it was possible to escape some of the discrimination. Geoffrey was often dismissive about the Irish and it embarrassed me in company. I would be taking a big risk to have him meet my family as rural Ireland was still poor, with no running water. He would have difficulty believing how people coped with the sanitation in rural areas.

I always liked to go home on my own so that I could spend quality time with my nieces and nephews and be part of a family. I just loved taking my nieces and nephews on donkey rides on the farm, which was a lot of fun. I was reliving my own childhood. There was always great excitement at Easter time and it gave me great pleasure to bring Easter eggs; no small one would be appreciated. I was in my mid-thirties and was very restless; wandering around the world like a headless chicken. I went home on holiday and my auntie said to me: "Aren't you the lucky one that did not get married?" I was really shocked as I did not think that I was past marriage age. I always looked much younger than my age and enjoyed being with younger, modern company.

I lived for my holidays; my sister Alma and I went on a hitchhiking/youth hostelling tour to Belgium, Holland, Germany, and Luxemburg. We had an amazing time and met lovely people, even though we had no idea of the local languages. One day there was a queue outside the labour exchange which was near the bank. We needed money and joined the queue thinking it was the bank. Then a fellow tried to lure us to some backward area but luckily we copped on in time. Being Irish, most people had a great welcome for us. One night in Frankfort we went to a hamburger stall and when the owner heard that we were Irish he took us to his home to meet his wife and family. They treated us to dinner and German entertainment and gave us accommodation for the night.

Arabian Tales

By 1978/9 I was getting itchy feet again and in need of some excitement. Saudi Arabia was recruiting for staff at the time and there were other girls going, so I did not need much encouragement. I applied, went for the interview and was accepted. Everybody thought that we were all mad as Saudi Arabia was a very strict Muslim country. Most people went for financial gain but that was the last thing on my mind. Change of scenery and love were uppermost on my mind. Having said that, I did put the money to good use later.

We arrived in Saudi Arabia not knowing what to expect. It was so arid with a vast expanse of sandy desert. The heat was intolerable at times and it was no relief to go into the sea, as it was like having a hot bath. There was air-conditioning in all the homes and workplaces. We were given accommodation on a temporary basis, which was very basic; often sharing a room with somebody on a different shift. The company which I worked for was an American/Saudi oil company called Aramco (Arab American Oil Company) which was started in 1933. It had its own camp and private area of beach which were not subjected to Saudi rules. Aramco's residential communities, with their well-tended landscaping, are often likened to suburbia in the US southwest of California. The proximity to the gulf guaranteed that boating, fishing and swimming would become favourite sports. Most of the European sports are available somewhere in Saudi Arabia, which reflects the international composition of the work force.

Our passports were kept by Personnel and if one wanted to leave the country, a visa had to be obtained. All kinds of entertainment were laid on in camp; including cinema, swimming pools and sports facilities. When we went out to the local town it was necessary to dress in a modest fashion, otherwise the religious police would pick us up and take us back to camp. Some areas of the Middle East were stricter and, if a man and woman who were not married were out together, they could be put in prison. The weather was so hot it was more comfortable to dress in long loose clothing during the day. Bus services were provided on camp to transport people to the supermarket and beach. Most of the Americans had their own cars and had been living there for longer periods. The Americans were well catered for, got most of the managerial jobs and had priority for the best accommodation. The salary was determined by the basic salary of the country of origin. There was a large amount of nursing staff from India, other areas of Middle East and the Philippines. For doing the same job we all got different salaries. We had an orientation period and were assigned to our different areas.

I had done general nursing for some time and was expecting to do the same there. They were opening up a new Psychiatric Unit and I was informed that I would be assigned to it. I expressed some reservations as I did not speak the language, but I was reassured that classes were available to teach Arabic. I was pleased and delighted to learn a new language. There were also plenty of interpreters; some people from other areas of the Middle East had been there for years and spoke the language fluently. This did reassure me and I was sent to Arabic classes free of charge, which I thoroughly enjoyed. We did not learn to write Arabic as most of the documentation was in English. I already had a little knowledge from working in the private clinic in London.

In most countries dress is influenced by the climate, utility and custom. In Saudi Arabia there are a few minor regional exceptions; usually slight variations or additions to the basic garment. Boys and men wear the *thaub*: a loose fitting white shirt. They also wear headgear called *ghutrah*, which is red and white in colour. The ladies wear floor length black clothing when out in public but beneath they wear nice colourful clothes when visiting friends or in female company.

Arab women were not allowed to drive. Western women were allowed to drive but only on campus. I did my driving test and am the proud owner of a Saudi Arabian driving licence. When I came to Ireland on holiday I was stopped by the guards and asked to produce my licence. When the guard looked at it he did not know what to say as it was written in Arabic. He told me that I was not allowed to drive here on that licence but I informed him that it was current and, as I was on holiday, it was perfectly legal. He accepted this and I was allowed to drive on.

Saudi Arabian men and women rarely socialised together. Some of the men wore western clothes, particularly when they were going abroad. Many owned property in the major capital cities of the world and were very rich; others lived very ordinary lives. There was a big population of native Arabs working for the company. They were well supported financially and given loans to build housing if they lived off camp. They became very rich very quickly. Some of the Europeans were rather critical and would say that they went from "camel to Cadillac" in too short a space of time, with no transition period. Westerners tried to impose their ideas on to them, as has happened in other cultures, which often met with resentment.

The native indigenous people are called *Bedouin* or *Bedu*. They are nomadic camel breeding tribes of the Arabic desert. They travel all over the Middle East and live in tents. They trade and breed in camels. Large prices could be obtained from the rulers and richer merchants for thoroughbred camels. Some tribes made money from carrying goods across the desert. In the desert, the Bedu need very little to keep themselves alive. Their herds provide them with food and drink. They have certain requirements which they cannot supply themselves, such as cloth, cooking pots, knives, ammunition, occasional loads of dates and grain and such luxuries as coffee or tobacco. To get those things they visited markets in the villages or towns and sold a camel or goat, water skins, rugs or saddlebags.

The discovery of oil brought enormous wealth to the Saudi Arabian Bedu, who love money. They could earn large sums of money by guarding a dump, or by doing work which was certainly easier than watering thirsty camels on a nearly dry well in the middle of the summer. They had plenty of food, abundant sweet water and long hours of sleep. They seldom had these things before, and were now being paid into the bargain. Their love of freedom and the restlessness that was in their blood drew most of them back to the desert, where life was becoming more difficult.

For the western population the social life was good; there were companies from all over the world working on projects to build up the infrastructure of Saudi Arabia. The overseas companies could not operate on their own but had to have a Saudi partner; they had a 49/51% partnership in favour of the Saudis. Most of the professional expertise was provided by the western population. Manual labour was provided by employees from the Third World. They were very subservient and not treated very fairly. There was little employment in their own countries and they were prepared to put up with any treatment just to get work to provide for their families back home. Their accommodation was very basic, overcrowded and of poor standard. Some had paid recruitment fees in their own countries and had to work for several months to pay it off. Some were unable to cope with being away from their families and ended up receiving psychiatric care. They were repatriated when their condition permitted. I always treated them with great compassion, which they appreciated. Some nurses were sent to escort them and hand them over to their families, with no compensation or follow up treatment. They reminded me of Irish people who had emigrated and experienced similar difficulties.

If a US employee became ill they were sent back to US for treatment and returned when they had recovered. Europeans were treated fairly well but did not enjoy the same perks or privileges as the Americans. Very few overseas nurses were in senior positions at this time. Many of the rich Saudis had domestic help from the Third World and it was alleged that their treatment and conditions were not acceptable. They had to comply with their employers wishes and were often sexually exploited. They were so desperate for money to feed their families that they tolerated a lot of unfair treatment. The employer held their passports and they could not change employment. There was no agency to monitor employment conditions and if an employee did not comply, the next step was deportation and a ban on re-entering the country. Offending the Saudis or their culture was unacceptable.

Western employees socialised together, mixing in their own circles just to meet up with other expatriates, particularly girls. We burned the candle at both ends and often had narrow shaves with the law and culture. One time we went to a party outside camp and were collected by a person who was new to the country. Most of the road network appeared the same. Unless you knew where you were going it was difficult to negotiate your way; particularly at night. The weather was so hot we wore very light party dresses. On one particular occasion the designer of my dress had been a bit economical with material. It was asymmetrical knee length and slit up the thigh; I had no jacket or cardigan. The fellow who was driving us could not find the way to our accommodation and drove around for hours; eventually he gave up and took us back to his hotel. We all slept in his room, which was strictly forbidden. Next morning we had to climb over a wall (not so easy as I was wearing very high heels) as we could not go out the front door. I cannot imagine what my charge would be: dress not in keeping with the tradition, post inebriated state or mixing with the opposite sex. This was a very lucky escape as people were put into prison for less.

Another time there was a curfew on camp and nobody inside knew about it. Security on the gate was strict and non-residents had to have a valid reason to get in. Needless to say the expatriates were very nice to the security men and I can imagine some "Baksheesh" (tips) exchanged hands.

There was a lot of political unrest in the Middle East at this time. Censorship was very strict and there was very little news about the outside world. The news broadcasts were edited and only news favourable to the country was delivered. There were no magazines so as not to contaminate the minds of the local people. Most were strict Muslims. For adultery or any serious crime there would be a public flogging on a certain day of the month in the open square. If someone stole they were likely to have an arm cut off; this was a great deterrent so the crime rate was very low. One girl, who was hurt by a man, said that it was a pity the same law did not apply to westerners and it would not be the arm that was cut off.

Nurses and all females were in great demand and men were anxious to have a contact within the camp to avail of the social life. Legally there was no alcohol allowed in the country as it was strictly Muslim, but this law was regularly broken. Some Europeans had their own breweries and produced large amounts of alcohol, which was quite lucrative. The drink was called *Sikiki*, which means "friend" in Arabic. I can tell you it was no friend because if it was not given enough time to brew the hangover would be dreadful. It was sold to contacts and for a high price. The quicker the turnover the more lucrative it became and people became very greedy. Most people made their own wine and brewing kits and products were freely available. Sometimes it was necessary to get ingredients brought in from outside the state to make a better brew. I was often complimented about the red wine which I produced. People were taking a great risk as those caught smuggling in drink or brewing it were put in prison. The rich Arabs had their contacts and were able to obtain real alcohol. Americans also got in alcohol by diplomatic or other means. Some people took advantage of the locals and would dilute the local brew with tea to make it look like whiskey. They accepted this as some had never tasted whiskey. Some came over to get away from alcohol, only to find sadly that there was a lot more drinking and more free time to do it.

There were far more men than women and most men were not allowed to bring their families out, with the exception of the Americans. European men had single contracts and had their fares paid home every four months. They could bring their families over for holidays. Those contracts were for Europeans mainly, other countries had different conditions. Some of the men who lived outside camp were living in single male accommodation which they did not find satisfactory. They found life very frustrating not having access to female company. Men often lied about their marital status and the usual story was "my wife does not understand me" or "we are separated"; which was not a lie, technically speaking.

Some girls were very gullible and lived with some of those men hoping that there would be a future in the relationship. It was difficult to know which the men liked best; the woman or her nice accommodation. Consequently there were many broken hearts as, when the contract ended so did the relationship. The men led the girls along saying that they were not sure, but as soon as they left they had no problem making their minds up. Contact was severed when they left the country.

Secondly, girls who were never accustomed to much attention became too easily available and fell for a lot of sob stories. One male friend said that it was obvious that I was accustomed to attention from the opposite sex, as I did not fall for any sob stories. There were some good characters who said that they were "there for a good time, not a long time." They had a very liberal attitude to casual relationships. One Irish character would get rather inebriated and go to girls saying that he had a "tingling in his groin." One girl had an encounter with a fellow who she described as a pole vaulter because of his agility and versatility in the bedroom. Sometime later she saw him on the beach with a woman and child.

When I went there first I was not really interested in a relationship as there were plenty of activities and also plenty of company in the nurses' residence. At a party I was introduced to Bruce, a fellow from the UK and we went out together for two and half years. I discovered that it was necessary to have an escort as some of the men did not behave very well towards female company; at least not in a manner that would be entertained at home. They often talked about girls in a very uncomplimentary way. It was difficult to sort out the wheat from the chaff. One of my friends described some of the men as being like octopuses.

Bruce had a shared partnership in a boat and we went camping and participated in water sports with a crowd of friends. I was often the only female with several fellows. When I drove the boat for the water skiers I was told that I looked like a Bond girl. There were some very amusing characters in the group and one fellow would "moon" for fun, just to distract the skier. No one who knows me could ever imagine that I would participate in such activities.

It was so beautiful sitting around a big open fire under the light of the moon on a warm night. Many times a joint of weed would be produced and everybody had a drag. I often had a drag and unlike Bill Clinton I did inhale it. I found it very relaxing and it gave a great feeling of well-being. There were plenty of the locally produced refreshments and we had lots of fun singing, joking and having a midnight swim. It was also beautiful waking up in the morning on the beach and looking at the still peaceful blue sea. There was a feeling of peace and tranquillity; a well-earned release from the shift pattern, which was very difficult.

The Americans got their shift of choice and did mainly day shift to suit their family life. The shifts were: week one, 7am to 3pm; next week 3pm to 11pm and the third week 11pm to 7am, with days off in between to cover the monthly period. It was very disorientating and when you woke up you often did not know which shift you were on, or if it was a day off. They were very strict about sick leave and got wise to the fact that nurses would call in sick if they wanted to go to a party. Consequently, if you did not feel well, you had to present at casualty to be certified sick by a doctor. There was always some colleague on duty who would give a nod to the Doctor and sick leave was granted. With that barrier out of the way, the next worry was that nobody would be at the party to spill the beans. There were a lot of barbeques and the outdoor life was very enjoyable. There were always an excuse to have a party, and every small event was celebrated.

I really had a very enjoyable nursing position and I loved the patients as they were so simple and pleasant. Most of the time I worked with a Lebanese male nurse called Gazi. There were nurses from other Third World countries. We had a good working relationship and the patients were always pleased when we were on duty. One day an American nurse was very strict with one of the patients. They reported her to the Consultant and he was not too happy with her approach. He specifically stated that there was no complaint about me. I had more understanding of the rural people and they also responded well to me. Most did not speak English but they really enjoyed my speaking Arabic to them. I did have fun with the language. I had occasion to give directions to a female patient, which she did not like. When her son came in to visit she told him about the incident he said in Arabic "never mind her Mama, she is English." I replied in Arabic that I was not English. He got a bit of a surprise but we both laughed and shook hands. Another time a male Arab speaking colleague was writing his nursing report. He asked me "how you spell mastication?" I spelled another word with similar spelling but a very different meaning. (mast—bation). I tried to enlist the support of another English speaking colleague but my Arabic colleague knew the difference.

When we went to the local town shopping whenever Arabic was spoken they were so flattered and pleased; it did help with getting a good bargain in jewellery. They really liked the Irish and it was the time of the hunger strikes in Northern Ireland. Of course they were very well versed on the situation. Most spoke little English but would say "Bobby Sands" the name of one of the hunger strikers. They likened the Palestinian/Israeli conflict to the one in Northern Ireland. Many of the Palestinians who were evicted from their homeland worked and settled there. I heard many disturbing stories about their lives and the details of their evictions. Their lands and properties were confiscated by the Israelis to build new settlements for people coming from other areas of the world. They were often asked to leave their homes on a temporary basis and return when the conflict was settled. Sadly they never did return and made their lives in other areas of the Middle-East. I was working with a Palestinian male nurse when President Anwar Sadat of Egypt was assassinated.

Apparently he had signed some agreement with the US that was not favourable to Palestinians. My colleague was jubilant and expressed no sadness for his loss.

Many of the people I looked after had never had any contact with western people, as many of them came from the desert and were of the Bedouin culture. Having being brought up in rural Ireland I could identify with their simplicity. They were fascinated with our way of life. They would never have discussed anything of an intimate nature with anybody, but felt secure to do so with a stranger in a professional setting, knowing it was confidential. The ladies were very curious to learn about the lives of western women. One day I was sitting slumped on a seat with my feet on a coffee table, probably nursing a hangover. The ladies were sitting around me giggling and asking questions of an intimate nature. The Director of Nursing paid a surprise visit. I stood up rather quickly and he said "stay where you are, that's the best psychiatry I have seen for some time. They could not understand how women had sex before marriage or cohabitated. If that happened in Saudi Arabia they would be stoned or killed. Little did they know about the exploits of some of their men folk, who travelled to sex capitals of the world. Previously, when I worked at a private clinic in London, I nursed patients who were terminally ill and were referred to top consultants in London, paid for by the Saudi government. They were given steroid treatment which gave them a feeling of well-being. They would get permission to go out to town and say that they were going to Victoria, (they called it Fuctoria). Judging by the smile on their faces, the obvious conclusion was that they had not been out to buying souvenirs.

I was equally interested in learning about their culture. The indigenous population did not marry outside their culture, religion, tradition or location. All of the marriages were arranged and it was necessary to have a large dowry. The dowry consisted of camels and the more camels a man had, the better match he got for his daughter. When babies were born male children were the most welcome, as the father did not have to worry about the dowry.

The hospital catered for employees, their families and relatives. Most of the influential Arabs went overseas for private treatment. There was great family support and families came for miles to visit daily. They suffered the same kind of psychiatric difficulties as western people. They were very strict Muslims and prayed four times per day. It is the duty of every Muslim to go to Mecca on pilgrimage at least once in their lifetime. During this period Muslims have to observe a fasting period and not eat or drink between sunrise to sunset. Europeans have to respect their tradition and not be seen eating or drinking in public; the religious police monitored this and would remind you if you happened to forget.

According to their religion, men are allowed to have more than one wife. Some women accepted this as part of their culture, but others reacted badly to another addition to the family. Wives had their different roles and positions and it often worked well. They could never understand why I was not married and said that I would have lovely children. I would joke to them in Arabic that I had murdered three husbands, which greatly amused them particularly because my Arabic was not fluent. Some European girls did date the Arab men and were rewarded with generous amounts of gold and gifts.

The Lebanese in particular, were very suave but most married within their own culture and had arranged marriages. They still liked to have a fling with European girls. Lebanon had been a French colony for some time and most spoke fluent French and had all the finesse of French people. The population was mixture of Christian and Muslim. It was the leisure centre of the Middle East. Because of its proximity to Palestine/Israel freedom fighters made their base in Lebanon and brought it into a war zone. The country was devastated, particularly the capital city of Beirut. Lebanese people were very angry to be brought into a conflict which was no concern of theirs and were often hostile to Palestinians. Many Irish soldiers were deployed there, working with the UN peacekeeping forces to monitor the situation. Therefore the Lebanese had great respect for the Irish.

I had several invitations from Arabic men but declined them all. Relationships were difficult enough for me without the added complication of culture and religious divide. One girl was dating a Lebanese man for some time. He went on holiday and when he came back he told her that he had got married. The marriage had been arranged by both families. Needless to say she was shocked and very upset. There was an article in the Irish newspapers saying that some Irish girls were involved in a prostitution ring in some part of Saudi Arabia. This greatly upset most of the well-behaved Irish nurses and they wrote a letter to the newspaper denying that this was happening. One western girl dated one of the many Saudi princes. When she terminated the relationship she was put under house arrest and deported promptly without being given any choice.

Travels through The Middle East, Asia, Australia

We got six weeks annual leave with our flights home paid for. The fare money could actually be used to do any combination of trips. Travel agents were very knowledgeable and would arrange trips to anywhere in the world. If the fare money was not sufficient for the trip more money could be added. They were also very helpful about getting visas and advising on the different requirements of the different countries. Many people went on short breaks to Bahrain, which at the time was more liberal than Saudi Arabia. America and Britain had military interests there. It was the shortest known flight, just 10 minutes flying time. There was also a Dhow or small boat which provided frequent service.

One trip we went on was to India, travelling to Bombay, Delhi and Kashmir. There were many museums and monuments, including the Taj Mahal. Part of the trip we stayed on a house boat, which may sound exciting but it was a very shabby affair and they were very economic with the food. The poverty was incredible and children were often maimed and put out on the street to beg; which was very upsetting. We happened to be passing a big wedding in Bombay and got invited in to share in the reception. The upsetting thing was that outside this lavish affair there were people starving for food and not offered any. We were invited in to show us the famous Indian hospitality.

Being a tourist one had to be on your guard, otherwise you got ripped off. At the hotels the staff were very eager to help with travel arrangements. One girl gave her ticket to a hotel employee to confirm the booking. When she got to the airport there was no reservation and her seat had been cancelled; obviously sold. She had to purchase another ticket.

In the summer of 1980 I went home to Ireland to spend some time there. There was always great excitement when I was coming as I brought gifts to order. I always had a great affinity for children and really enjoyed my nieces and nephews. It was very exciting for them to have an auntie working in the Middle East and bringing home gifts which were different. They once said that their auntie should be Miss World!

The Irish summer was like the Middle East winter; so I did not do too much sunbathing. Getting a good summer in Ireland you have to make the best of the sunshine. I went on a trip around Ireland with a friend, Maura and my sister, Alma. They wanted to sunbathe and enjoy the sun but I was feeling cold and wanted to keep travelling. Music cassettes were very cheap and everybody topped up their tape collection. I brought a tape recorder/radio centre for the children which caused great excitement; the children were able to tape themselves talking and singing.

Despite my home-sickness I was always pleased to return to the Middle-East, as that was where my home was at the time. Somebody said that I must be the only person who looked forward to returning to Saudi Arabia, as many were there not out of choice but out of financial necessity

The next trip was to Israel and Jordan. There was political unrest in Israel and friends were advising us not to go; small things like that did not deter my friend Kate and me. We went on conducted tours around Israel, the Holy Land and a trip to the Dead Sea. The tour guide was very selective about the information he gave. We passed Palestine detention camps and no information was given on that part of the tour. It was an amazing trip as, when I was a child I thought that Israel was in heaven and I couldn't believe that I was there in person. I was a bit disillusioned as some things were only presumed - e.g. the stable where the baby Jesus was born. Even though there were political problems the main tourist areas were safe. The security was very strict and every item was meticulously checked. Palestinian people had a hard time and security services made it difficult and frustrating for them to move from one area to the other. We had to get special stamps on our passports as officially Israel did not allow access to some countries of the Middle East, but made an exception for tourists. The Dead Sea is 420 metres below sea level, between Israel and Jordan. It is rich in minerals and a swim was very therapeutic for us weary travellers

We proceeded to Jordan, spent some time in the capital city Amman and did some sightseeing there. As western women we had to be careful to stay in public areas; otherwise we would get unwanted attention from the opposite sex. We proceed to Petra, Jordan's most famous ancient wonder. Carved out of soaring sandstone rock this "rose city, half as old as time," with its magical tombs and temples is without doubt the most remarkable sight in the Middle East.

A nomadic Arab community, in search of a home hidden from the outside world, chose Petra as their capital, after uncovering several springs in the region. From their new home they set up a lucrative water-cum-protection racket for passing caravans on the Silk route, amassing huge wealth from the thriving trade in spices and incense. As highly skilled architects they devoted their spare time to sculpturing temples and tombs out of sheer rock, with elaborate columned facades and intricate designs on par with those in ancient Athens and Rome. The city's glory reached its peak around the time of Jesus, until the trade routes changed direction after the collapse of the Roman Empire and the city fell into decline. For centuries few ever knew of Petra's existence, but in 1812 a young Swiss traveller heard talk of a beautiful city lost in the Wadi Musa mountains. He disguised himself as an

Arab and uncovered Jordan's jewel for the rest of the world to see. After exploring the impressive chambers, the inner sanctuary of the Treasury which once served for a Nabaataen king, we headed towards the centre of the city along the Street of Facades to the breath-taking 6,000 seater amphitheatre. In the same area was a sprawling city of tombs, a market place, palaces and Byzantine churches; a legacy of the Romans who settled there in the 2nd century AD.

After each trip I was always refreshed and looked forward to going back to work. This was where my life was. Once when I returned from holiday the patients were standing outside the office. I asked them what was wrong and they said that they thought that I had left and that they would not see me again. That was very flattering and indicated the rapport I had established with them. My relationship with Bruce ended and I was feeling restless and lost. I was finding the shift system very monotonous, tiring and was very unhappy. I befriended some Australian fellows through mutual acquaintances and maintained a good social life. Bob, one of the Australians left and invited me to visit. I planned a trip with stopovers at Singapore and Hong Kong. At this time Hong Kong was still under British Rule but was subsequently returned to China in 1997. I did all the sightseeing trips and went to Macao, a Chinese Island just off Hong Kong, which was very primitive and interesting. Going on organised trips it was easy to meet other people. I bought silk and found the adventure very interesting.

I then went to Thailand and spent some time in Bangkok, which was an amazing city full of culture. The architecture was so different from the Middle-East and there were so many temples and places of worship. I had not heard good reports about this city as there is a very sleazy element; it was the sex capital of the East. Most of the men worked in the Middle-East and as a result, there were far more women than men. The economy was poor.

From a very early age ladies worked in massage parlours and other leisure areas just to get money to feed their families. Prostitution was legal and practised openly. I found it disturbing to see older men with very young girls; later known as sex tourists. Men from Saudi Arabia and other areas went there for weekends, not to see the temples or explore the culture. They usually returned with a smile on their faces and a few days later they visited their GP for obvious reasons.

I went on an overnight trip by bus to Chang Mai, which is up north of the country. There was a tribe living there with their own traditional dress and customs. As I was travelling on my own I was restricted to where I would go because of safety issues, so I had to go on conducted tours and stay in safe areas. Crime is very low there as punishment is severe for offenders. It was a country that did not attract the best kind of people. As a female travelling alone I had to be conscious of this.

When I arrived in Perth, Bob had not expected me to avail of his invitation and was a bit surprised that I was actually there. People say all kinds of things when they are desperate and he was trying to win my affection when he was in Saudi. He lived in a house with English girls and they were very pleasant and accommodating; involving me in their social activities. I did sightseeing trips around Perth. One interesting trip was to an Aboriginal reservation. It was very interesting to hear about their culture and difficulties. When I got back I told the girls where I had been; they had never known that there was a reservation. Despite all those difficulties I really enjoyed the trip and was rejuvenated for a short time.

On my return to Saudi Arabia I befriended another Australian, Andrew. It was necessary to have a companion to go to parties and functions in order to ward off unwanted attention from the needy men. He was much younger than me but we got on very well and had similar interests. He loved to travel and was also bitter about a relationship he had had in Australia. He could not have found a more experienced person to deal with broken relationships. I was becoming an expert by this time.

At weekends we went on trips to the desert and visited the Bedouin areas. I really enjoyed this as they were so pleased to hear a western woman speaking their language and they were very amused. Their way of life was very interesting. They lived in massive tents and cooked big meals on an open fire. There were different tents for women and men and socially they did not interact. They would cook a large goat on the fire and all sit around on the sand and enjoy a large feast. They had no cutlery and ate with their left hands, this was for religious reasons, the right hand was considered unclean due to being used for toilet purposes. They were very welcoming and offered food and "chai" (black tea) served in small cups to all who visited.

We then travelled to the port of Hofuf, which is a port used for years to trade spices from the Far East. We were both interested in exploring more of the Middle East and travelling across the desert to the Empty Quarter. The Empty Quarter is in the southern part of Saudi Arabia known as Rub al Khali. It is 750 miles long and has a maximum width of 400 miles. It covers an area of 240,000 square miles and is bigger than France, Belgium and Holland altogether. It is the largest continuous body of sand in the world. The sands are not all of one type. Most of the time the Empty Quarter is uninhabited; except during the rainy season when the Bedouins move in to take advantage of the rich pasture. I found the culture fascinating and was eager to explore more. Our freedom to do this was compromised by the fact that male and female are not allowed to travel together unless they are married, which was disappointing.

I was still restless and unable to settle and decided that it was time to move on. Where else to go only London? I had reservations about leaving as I enjoyed my nursing position so much and really enjoyed the Arabic culture. I looked at advertisements in the Nursing Press and saw a position for a Sister in a private clinic. I applied and got a reply inviting me for interview on my return to London. I resigned my position with some reluctance in April 1982 as I was ready for a change.

Of course there was the usual great celebrations and we had a few farewell parties; any excuse for a get-together. My Lebanese work colleague, Gazi, threw a big party which was enjoyed by all. There was also a party from colleagues at work and other friends. I was really sad leaving as I had developed a great affinity for the Arabic people. There was so much more to learn about their culture and traditions but as a single woman there were too many restrictions.

London Calling (Again)

I went home to Ireland for a short break while waiting for my luggage to arrive in London. Needless to say my visits provided great excitement as there were presents for all. When I arrived in London I stayed temporarily with my brother, John and joined a Nursing agency, which I had previously worked for. There were vacancies at the Women's Prison in Holloway Road and I was offered a position there. I was excited about this as I always had an interest in Prison work. Initially when I got there I was surprised, as the building was old and very basic; so different from my previous hospital. The hospital in Saudi Arabia was new and modern. After a short time I settled in and found it very challenging. The staff there encouraged me to make application for full-time work, which I was interested in doing. Unfortunately they did not have live-in accommodation and the distance was too far to travel, so for that reason I had to decline the offer.

I contacted the private clinic as instructed, where I had made application prior to returning to London. I was invited for interview and offered the position. The new building where the vacancy arose would not be opening for some time, which did not suit me. I needed a secure job with live-in accommodation as my plan was to purchase property and I needed a mortgage. As a last resort I contacted the private clinic where I had previously worked and got a position with live-in accommodation. It was not the career move which I had planned but beggars can't be choosers and I had to do it for practical reasons. I requested permanent night duty as I had plans to work there for only a short period.

I was 38 years old and had no permanent base. Most people who went to Saudi Arabia purchased property when they returned to UK, which appeared to be the natural progression. This was exciting and I went to an estate agency for information and advice. I saw a few properties and was not too impressed for various reasons. The prospect of owning a house was exciting but also daunting. There was no property boom at this time but, fortunately for me, this occurred soon afterwards.

A nice property came on the market in a very sought after area. The estate agent wanted to view the property for her own information. When I got there I was really impressed, but it was way out of my price range and, in addition to getting a mortgage, all my savings would be eaten up. It was within walking distance of a sports centre and swimming pool, which was of interest to me. It was the only house on the street that had mature trees in the front garden, which was appealing. The garden was very private and not over-looked. The owners were emigrating and were eager so sell so my agent suggested that I put in an offer. I did this at a greatly reduced price and, after some bargaining and their urgency to sell, my offer was accepted. A few days later my solicitor phoned to tell me that there was a higher bidder and asked if I could up my offer. I could not do this as I was financially stretched to my limit. I informed him of this and he said that he would try to negotiate. He came back and was pleased to say that my offer had been accepted. The main advantage was that I was a cash-buyer, had no chain and the deal could go through quickly.

I was really excited with my business acumen but had no one there to share my delight. I phoned my sister, hoping that she would be pleased for me, but was so disappointed that she did show much enthusiasm. I was expecting to her to be delighted that I had finally got some roots, but good news or success was not celebrated in my family. I also purchased a cheap second-hand car which I needed mainly to go to work.

I continued to work permanent nights. Some of the friends that I had known had moved on and it was difficult to get into a social scene. I kept busy going to movies and theatre and trying to establish a social scene; but living abroad and working nights it is not so easy and the effort was becoming monotonous. One day I got a call from my Australian friend, Andrew, who had come to London from Saudi Arabia. We had shared interests and had established a good platonic friendship in Saudi Arabia. Getting into new relationships was becoming a drag but I was always optimistic that eventually there would be a positive outcome. He was staying with his friend, which coincidentally was in the same area where I had purchased my house. Soon afterwards all the legalities were completed on the new property and I got the key to move in. It sounded so exciting but when I opened the door I got such a feeling of isolation, loneliness and no one to share the responsibility. I felt like closing the door and running away. I had always lived in nurses' accommodation and there was always somebody to talk to if necessary. It even occurred to me to keep my room in the nurses' residence in case I could not cope with living alone. Luckily my friend Andrew was nearby and was always very helpful. My first instinct was to go out the back door for toilet purposes. I was thinking of home - we grew up without an indoor toilet. It is amazing the little things that are embedded in the subconscious, even though I had left home twenty years earlier.

Andrew helped me to move in to my own property and I made full use of my 90ft garden. The farming instinct never left me and I planted lettuce, carrots, parsnips, beetroot and cabbage, all organically grown, just for the challenge. There were also apple and pear trees. The garden was well kept and had lots of mature trees and plants. The gardener who had worked for the previous owner came looking for work. I was amused that I was moving into such good circles. I did not employ him as I was excited about the challenge of doing it myself; also my budget did not permit it. It was all very private and quiet as the area was residential. I loved flowers and spent many pleasurable moments gardening and sunbathing. Together with Andrew I had a big housewarming party and I enjoyed being the hostess. It was also an opportunity to show off my culinary skills, as I had done when abroad.

I was never a materialistic person and I just purchased the essentials – beds, fridges and some items of furniture from DIY stores. Some minor work had to be done and, as Andrew was an engineer he offered it to do it in exchange for accommodation. The excitement was short lived when the bills started to come in; my salary was not adequate to fulfil my financial obligations. I had to think quickly and decided to rent out rooms. I advertised and discovered that there was a great shortage of good accommodation. The arrangement was that we shared the kitchen; otherwise it was strictly business. I often hosted a dinner party for some social interaction with the tenants otherwise we all led our own lives. I was very lucky to get trustworthy tenants; it was also company in the house and somebody to keep an eye on the place when I was away. It worked out well and I had no difficulty with the arrangements. When I advertised I was very selective about the type of person I chose and that they respected the conditions of the agreement. I was taking a risk but I was a fairly good judge of character: if they satisfied the criteria by having a responsible job and were well-spoken they would be accepted. My first lodger stayed for about three years and I rarely had a vacancy. It was a great interest and I loved running my own little business. I had the offer of an arranged marriage from one of my eastern tenants which was unusual at the time.

Then the inevitable happened and Andrew and I started a relationship. It was never my intention but I guess the friendship grew and, practically it worked out well. We were both in need of love, affection and companionship and we had shared interests. We had a good social life and went to all kinds of entertainment, from punk rock to classical concerts, theatre and folk sessions. I remember booking tickets for theatre; usually first night has reduced prices. When we got there the red carpet was out with plenty of spectators. I had not realised that first night was also for invited stars and critics. I did not see anybody famous; having been away I did not recognise any of the TV stars. It was happy and it was nice to have somebody to share mutual interests. I felt safe and secure.

Having a property in London it was not too difficult to attract Australian friends. They always appeared to be travelling on a budget despite being very affluent at home. It was my first home and I was really enjoying playing house. I did not want too much intrusion, much to Andrew's dissatisfaction. I was in no financial position to subsidise travellers.

We were both interested in travelling. He purchased a BMW motorbike and our first trip was camping to Scotland. It was in the month of October, not the best time to go north. As I was on permanent nights my sleeping pattern was disrupted. I was falling asleep on the back of the bike as the motorway was so monotonous. We travelled all the way up to Inverness and to some of the islands, including the Mull of Kintyre, made famous by Paul McCartney. The weather was so cold for camping that we spent time in the pub and topped up with whiskey to warm us up so that we could get a good night's sleep. Travelling around Scotland was very enjoyable and the countryside is similar to Ireland in places. The people were very friendly and welcoming; there were very few tourists at that time of year so we were quite a novelty. The locals were surprised with our mode of transport.

We also went on a camping trip to the Forest of Dean in Gloucestershire, which is England's most ancient forest consisting of 27,000 acres of land. It was at Easter time and it was so delightful to hear the cuckoo. Having lived in cities for years, I had not heard this amazing sound since I was a child.

We were living together and getting along fine, it was my first experience of a family home life and I was really content. We hosted many parties and barbeques and were enjoying a good social life. I made my own wine, just for the challenge and it always appeared to go down well at parties.

My family was unaware of my arrangements. Many people lived together in London, which was not so in Ireland as people were very prudish and narrow-minded, particularly the rural people. Very few people in rural Ireland had telephones, which was great as I could live my life without too much interference. Soon afterwards my mother got a phone installed, which caused me some anxiety. Prior to this she was not aware of my activities and communication was by mail. She often rang asking my personal financial business and giving me advice as if she was qualified to do so. There is some difference in how life works in London compared to rural Ireland but she did not seem to realise this.

I was settled in my home and was getting tired of night duty. I decided it was time to concentrate on my career as I was not having much job satisfaction in my current position. I applied for a position in the NHS as a community nurse in the local area. I went for interview and the interviewee said that I had got a terrific reference from my employer in Saudi Arabia. He phoned me later and said that I was not successful for that post but offered me a position in the in-patient department. I was really chuffed and accepted it. The salary was very low but having the lodgers I could afford to take a drop in salary. I was anxious to get back to the NHS as promotional opportunities were better;

also job satisfaction greater and more secure. It took a while to settle into the different system. Having come from the private sector and the American system I found that things were less efficient. I was not always the most popular with the staff due to my different ideas and my efficiency, but got used to it eventually.

Andrew was still unemployed; there were few engineering positions in the UK and competition was keen. Luckily he got a good job in the South of England. I went with him to the interview. He got lost and thought that he had flat tyre. There were some Irishmen working on the road and he asked them if the wheel was flat. They replied: "No it is round." I was quite amused as he was not always complimentary about the Irish nation. Another day we were travelling on the train and there was a fellow countryman who was rather inebriated, on board. He was sitting beside an American lady and he said to her "are we near hic, hic, near Willesden Green?" She ignored him. He muttered to her: "Who the f---k do you think you are? Somebody from Madame Tussauds or what?" I interjected and said that I was getting off there and I would tell him. Andrew was not too happy that I had admitted to being Irish. It was not the best time to be Irish in London as the IRA had planted a bomb in Hyde Park and men and horses were killed.

During my holidays we did some travelling. One trip was to Scandinavia on the motorbike, covering Denmark, Sweden and Norway. When I told my colleagues at work that I was going on a motorbike they were surprised. Needless to say my family were not aware of my adventures. Even though it was summer it was quite cold in Norway. There was snow in some areas. We camped mostly but stayed in youth hostels if the weather was too cold. We were planning to go to North Cape but it was holiday time and there were plenty of caravans on the road. Also the roads were very narrow so we had to abandon that idea. There were families everywhere and it was then that my biological clock started ticking, the desire to have a family was overwhelming. I had such lovely memories of my nieces and nephews and was always so lonely when I returned to an empty house. I discussed it with my girlfriend who was a midwife and she said 'what is stopping you?' I had the house, the man and was financially secure. I just wanted to settle in one place, the nesting instinct was hitting me.

The main obstacle was as usual, My Mother! I discussed this issue with my friend and she was so surprised that my mother had such influence on my life. She suggested that I should go ahead and ignore her, that she would be dead and gone and that it would be too late for me. I then had to put the matter to Andrew. We had never discussed having a family and it was always his wish to return to Australia. I put it to him and he was not too enthusiastic but said that he would get back to me. He was enjoying all the perks of the relationship, having dinner cooked, his washing done, no responsibilities with mortgage or any financial issues. He was free to go and travel whenever he wished without having any commitment. He was very cynical about love and thought compatibility was more important.

I was content enough but time was not on my side; and I was becoming preoccupied with having a baby. I had always dreamed of having a daughter. I had been travelling around the world and was getting tired of the nomadic lifestyle. I wanted to establish roots. Going to Australia would mean getting a new job, a new driving licence and all that it takes to get established in a new country. My desire was always to return to Ireland. I made it quite clear that if he did not share my vision that he would have to leave my house. I also stated that if he fathered a child, I would not expect that he should change his plans and that I was prepared to bring the child up on my own. He told me if I felt that strongly about it, that I should start dating other people, but he still insisted that he was not moving. It was very frustrating for me as the property was mine and I was in a dilemma.

At that time I was getting some flattering attention from a very eligible doctor at work, but was not in a position to pursue it, as I had a live in partner. As sister on the ward I had plenty of occasions to interact with him, but I did not think that I would fit in with his social circles, due to being Irish and feeling so insecure. The first thing that always crossed my mind was bringing him home to meet my mother

We went on holiday to Turkey, travelling from Istanbul all along the Aegean coast on local transport and lived amongst the local people away from all the tourist areas. They were all very hospitable and we often stayed in family accommodation. It was very poor in some areas and families rented out rooms to subsidise their income. We travelled all along the coast and spent some time in different areas of interest, and then on to Gallipoli.

Four thousand Irishmen died there in 1915. They fought in British and ANZAC uniforms. Those who were fortunate enough to return arrived back to considerable ambivalence and even hostility about their role and sacrifice. They were denied the privilege of working in the public sector and were considered deserters. Mary McAleese, President of Ireland later visited Turkey and called for Ireland to hold a "shared commemoration" to mark the centenary of the beginning of the first World War in 2014 and also to restore their memory. She unveiled a plaque at Greenhill Cemetery to honour the memory of the Irish dead.

The sanitation was poor and toilet facilities were eastern style, it was not safe to drink the local water. It was a real holiday of escapism, as there were no UK papers available in the rural areas. The Miners' Strike was in progress and we did not known the details. We were staying in a B&B out in the country and in the morning I looked out the window to see cows grazing; for a moment I thought that I was back in Ireland. I sent a postcard to my friend in Ireland telling her of this and she was quite amused. The thought of returning to Ireland was never far away from my mind. There were too many obstacles; firstly the lack of employment and secondly my rather narrow-minded family. They were not aware of my cohabitating arrangements and if any of them rang, I would say that it was the lodgers who answered the phone.

After I returned to work I woke up one morning feeling very ill. I did not like to call in sick at such short notice and went to work. My temperature was fluctuating and I was very worried as I had not taken any malaria treatment. I had been lucky so far as I had never taken any health precautions prior to travelling, unless it was compulsory. I had to leave work and was becoming increasingly worried. I had the feeling that I was going to die or end up with some incurable disease. Next morning I went to my GP and gave him my history. I informed him where I had been on holiday. He was not my regular GP and he was really annoyed, saying that I should have known better being a nurse. He informed me that it could be malaria as that was one of the regions where it was prevalent. He referred me to an Infectious Diseases Hospital in London where the tests indicated that it was not malaria. The medical staff were concerned and decided to admit me for further investigations, as they were worried that no diagnosis was made.

I was in isolation and not allowed any visitors or contact with the outside world. Further tests were performed; all were negative except one which was inconclusive. A nurse discreetly asked me if I thought that I might be pregnant, which I thought was very unlikely. She then asked if I was, would I keep it. I was stunned as pregnancy never crossed my mind. I was unable to reply. The likely cause of my illness was urinary tract infection and I was discharged into the care of my GP. My GP did some tests and confirmed that I was indeed pregnant! I was so overjoyed. I could hardly speak. Andrew was not too happy but did not express any desire to leave. My friends were all so pleased and shocked in equal measure, as they thought that I was a career girl and did not want children. My friends from overseas were ringing to congratulate me. None of them had realized the secret that I had been harbouring for so long. The loneliness of not having my own family had always been on my mind. Material things and travelling have a very limited shelf life.

I kept well and had no ill effects from my pregnancy. I was so euphoric I probably would not have noticed if I had! Of course there was the chance that the baby might be abnormal due to my age. Older pregnant women are closely monitored, so that the mother has the choice to continue with the pregnancy in case there is any abnormality. I did not tell my mother and was waiting for confirmation that all was well. Luckily the results were all good.

Now it was time to face the music; tell my mother. I spent many hours planning what words I would use to minimise the shock. I rang and tried to ascertain the mood before hitting her with the news. I then said, "I have got some news" and she said, "What is that?" I told her that I was pregnant and, of course, she was shocked. She said, "Shure you are not married." I informed her about Andrew and our living arrangements. I asked her if she was disappointed, to which she replied, "you can say that" and hung up.

My sisters were supportive, although they were surprised at me for wanting a baby, as there was so much negativity about family life and having children in our family. There was a lot of media publicity about surrogacy at this time and I felt so privileged to be pregnant. My family always thought that travelling and having plenty of money was everything. I cannot imagine what my mother put my sisters through during this time; she started to have somatic aches and pains as a result of the stress. Of course they had to agree with her to keep the peace. She did not tell my father or brothers or any of the relations. I can imagine that they were very surprised that I was not going home, as I had usually visited every few months. It was hardly surprising that many girls would have chosen abortion, rather than having to deal with the attitude of my mother. She would not have to deal with the emotional trauma of such an act. She would have preferred to have known nothing about it.

The pregnancy was uneventful and I was in a state of euphoria most of the time, as I was feeling so well and felt lucky. I was very flattered when the patients collected to give me a present; most of them were on social security benefits. The patients always considered me very strict but very fair, which they appreciated. They were sad to see me go and wished me good luck. I did not know whether I was more excited about having a baby or leaving work. I worked up to five weeks before I went on maternity leave. It was July and it was a particularly hot summer. I adapted to my leisure time, sunbathing, listening to music and pottering around the garden. I was so tanned that when I went to hospital the staff thought that I had come back from some sunny climate. At the time *Frankie* by Sister Sledge was playing constantly on the radio; which now brings back lovely memories when I hear it. I had time to make contact with my friends and enjoyed watching tennis at Wimbledon on TV.

I had great care because of my age and was well monitored. As I was overdue my consultant decided to induce me. The delivery was normal and I delivered a baby girl without any painkillers or anaesthesia. My dream of having a daughter had come to pass.

The midwives were very surprised as they thought that I might have to have a caesarean section. Andrew was present most of the time. I was overwhelmed and overjoyed with my new responsibility. There were no mobile phones at that time. My first instinct was to share the wonderful experience with my mother and hope for her acceptance. Next day, when I got up, the first thing I did was to ring her to inform her of the good news. When I rang her she could not even say congratulations as there were members of the family present, including my father who had not been aware of the situation. As I spoke she kept saying "Yis, Yis." I was so happy that I completely overlooked her attitude.

I was discharged on July 13th 1985 when Live Aid was in full swing on the television. I lived near Wembley and was so happy sitting on the doorstep of my garden listening to the lovely music. I was very apprehensive initially, as I was afraid that I would not cope well with the responsibility of a new born without the support of the hospital or family. Secondly I was worried that I would get post-natal depression. Childbirth often brings out unpleasant emotions in vulnerable people. My friends and community nurse visited frequently and I adapted well settling into my new role of motherhood.

I could not believe the overwhelming joy I experienced when I became a mother. Nobody had told me about this aspect of motherhood. In my own family emotions were not verbalised. It was a shame that they had to suppress their joy at such a precious time. Andrea's arrival opened up a host of new emotions and responsibilities; my whole attitude to life changed. I would well up with emotion for little reasons. Watching a programme on TV about sick children, I was sobbing my heart out when my friend rang. She said, "are you crying?" I tried to cover up but she asked me if I was OK. She understood when I explained. The desire to nurture, protect and love unconditionally is very rewarding. I could never bear to hear my baby cry as I remembered as a child crying and being ignored. I enjoyed shopping and buying nice clothes and she always looked lovely. Andrew was feeling a bit out of joint as he was getting less attention than before. He had a shared partnership in a boat and he went sailing every weekend. I was happy to stay at home with my daughter; the nesting instinct overtook my desire to go sailing. He did not express any desire to leave his comfortable lifestyle and such matters were never discussed.

My two sisters, Mandy and Florence and their families came to visit; the nieces and nephews were delighted with their new cousin. They had good time and went to visit all the sights in London. When they went home I felt lonely and sad. Andrew's mother and uncle from Australia came to visit, which was great.

My father had been sick for some time, having mini-strokes. I was very emotional and thought that he was going to die without seeing his granddaughter. Coincidentally, she was born on his birthday. My mother had mellowed a bit at this stage, or so I thought. I rang to say that I wanted to go home before I returned to work. My mother was not in favour and used the excuse that they were modernising the house and that it was inconvenient. Probably she had not told the neighbours and relatives about the baby. My father instructed that the work cease and that I was to go home.

When I arrived home my father and I started crying. We were both so emotional and he was so happy for me. My mother never looked at the baby and was stomping around the house throwing everything out of her way, which was her usual behaviour. I overheard her telling a neighbour that she had never seen me so happy and that the baby was lovely; a pity she could not have communicated that to me. Some neighbours visited and never mentioned the baby; I was not aware that my mother had not informed them. She often said, "you don't need presents you got lots of money." Her preoccupation with money was very upsetting; she was so privileged to have such a healthy family which she took for granted.

I was very happy that I had gone home to see my father and considered the visit to be very worthwhile. It was lonely leaving my nieces and nephews, as they gave the baby great attention and I felt included in the family. Living in London, there were mother and toddler groups and it was easy to establish friendship and support with other mothers. There were local parks and activities laid on to entertain children. I was so content and proud to be a mother and enjoyed Andrea's daily progress. I spent time knitting and enjoyed making colourful zany cardigans and jumpers, which were greatly admired by friends.

Motherhood

Soon after I returned to London I was due back to work. I had arranged to work part-time. Working conditions were very family friendly and it was possible to work whatever hours suited. I set about looking for a child-minder and was lucky to find a very nice family. I was so apprehensive about leaving her as I had not been away from her for long periods. I went back to work and it was quite emotional; but it worked out fine as when I went to pick her up, she was so busy playing with the child-minder she hardly noticed me coming in. I was so pleased and relieved that she was well looked after and content.

Her development was very interesting. I had never been too interested in small babies but having my own was so different. I will never forget the first day when she smiled at me. Initially it was difficult as my sleeping pattern was disrupted due to teething problems and other childhood illnesses. I coped well as I only worked part-time. All was going well and I was enjoying family life. I then thought it was time to introduce Andrew to my family. The decision to do this was not without some apprehension and anxiety but it had to be done. I always loved going home at Easter time to see the new lambs and the countryside becoming alive with daffodils after a harsh winter. I had told Andrew of the great hospitality of the Irish people.

My family home had entertained all my in-laws and friends for years and I was expecting the same reception. We were staying at my sister's place, which was some relief as she had already met him when she was over. Unfortunately my father was in hospital at that time and we went to visit him. After the visit which was about three o'clock, my mother took us to a fast food café and said that it would save her from having to cook dinner. I was humiliated and neither of us ate dinner so early. She did prepare some salad for the evening meal. I had a splitting headache as every time I spoke she put me down or cut me short. She was asking personal questions about money and private affairs. Her favourite expression was: "Ye have yer money made."

My sister Florence babysat, which I really appreciated. Andrew and I went on a tour of Ireland. He was so impressed with the rugged scenery and the mountains. I was concerned about the lack of food and shelter for the newly born lambs due to the cold weather. We also went to the North of Ireland, which I was looking forward to as I had worked with many girls from Northern Ireland in my career and found them to be very friendly and funny. I had never been there before. All was going well until we were stopped by an armed Scottish soldier at the border asking us where we were going. He was pleasant but I couldn't accept being questioned by a foreigner in my own country. In 1985 there were very few non-Irish people in Ireland. The economy was very poor with more emigration than migration. There was no obvious border control at the point where we crossed and it came as a shock. It was usual procedure at the time to check all movements between North and South. We discovered that it was not the best time to be driving around in a UK registered car, as anything unusual would be viewed as suspicious.

I had thought that it would be great to get a good night's sleep and a break from motherhood. It was quite the contrary, after a few days I became very tearful and could not sleep at night. I knew Andrea was well looked after but I had never been away from her for such a long period. I just counted the time when I would resume my maternal duties again. I was trying to cover all this emotion up but was unable to do so. Andrew noticed how upset I was and said that we would cut the trip short if I desired, but I decided not to spoil his enjoyment.

Sophistication would not be the first thing that comes to mind when describing my mother! We had a big country kitchen and usually sat around the fire. There was no refuse collection and most recyclable things had to be burned. Peace would often be disturbed by a flying object past your ear in the form of a cardboard box or some other UFO. I was anxious about how my environmentally-friendly city partner would react. It was relief when we were on our way home as the tension was wearing me down.

Andrew was unsettled at work and said that he was going to leave. Not having financial obligations he was free to make a decision. For him the hills were always greener on the other side and it was difficult to humour him at times. I often had to inject some humour into situations to keep some harmony in the household. However he came home one day from work and said that he had given in his notice and his boss had offered him a job in Denmark. He said that he had accepted it without any consultation with me.

I was flabbergasted and asked him what was I to do. He told me that he wanted to keep his base in London, i.e. my home, and come back frequently. A concession on his contract was that they would pay for trips for the baby and me to go over. I thought about it for some time and wanted more clarity regarding our relationship. I put my cards on the table and said that if I was not included on his plan to go to Denmark, the relationship was over. He then agreed for Andrea and me to go also.

I packed my bags yet again, rented out my house, resigned from my job with great reluctance and decided to join him. I stored some of my property in the attic and kept my car in the garage, so the move was not as bad as previously. He stored most of his property and motorbike in my house also; life for him was pretty convenient and carefree. It did not occur to me to get leave of absence as it was always so easy to get work and I did not know how long the project would last. He went over to organise the accommodation and I went to Ireland for a holiday. My family thought my life was so exciting and appeared quite envious; little did they know what was going on behind the scenes. I was envious of their settled, comfortable lives.

I went to Copenhagen to join Andrew in June 1986. The apartment was beautiful and in the centre of town. At first the new adventure was exciting and I was enjoying spending time with my daughter. It was there she had her first steps, which was a great joy! I was fascinated with her development and she was changing and doing new things daily. However Andrew worked all day and I soon started to feel lonely and isolated as it was difficult to meet people. When he returned from work in the evenings he was tired and wanted to relax, which for me was very frustrating. I was in a dilemma and thought that if I got some part-time work it would help me to settle. I applied to a few places but it was a prerequisite that nurses be fluent in the native language, which eliminated me. Not speaking the language had its disadvantages as most of the signs and names were in Danish. I was afraid to go too far in case I would get lost. Most people had a conversational knowledge of English. It was a liberal society and most ladies went topless in the park during the summer months. It was so acceptable and if somebody was wearing a top, more attention was given to them. I met some women at the playground which helped somewhat.

I had heard that there was an Irish society which was hosting a St. Patrick's Day ball. We went to that and I made some friends. I met up with them and started to play badminton, which was a great outlet. I joined a sports facility and went swimming frequently. I hosted a few dinner parties for his work colleagues and made every effort to keep busy. But the relationship was deteriorating and life was becoming rather unpleasant. I guess that following the birth of my daughter, a lot of my buried childhood traumas were starting to surface and my behaviour was pretty unreasonable at times. Perhaps the milieu of family life was bringing some issues to the fore and I was acting like my mother; which must have been difficult to deal with! Being deprived of my full independence was also difficult.

Coincidently the lease on my house in London was up and I made a decision to return there after a period of ten months, Andrew stayed to complete his contract. I went to Ireland for a few weeks and then on to London. I was relieved and happy with my decision, thinking that the relationship was over. My family was not aware of any difficulties.

It was easier to make friends in London. I also had some friends there and there were great activities for mother and toddler. There was a drop-in centre provided free by the council and people spent a lot of time there. As with all things which are free, people were exploiting the system and the centre closed down, much to the disappointment of many needy parents. There were other play groups laid on for shorter duration. I was getting established and enjoying my lifestyle. I did not want to go back to work as I was enjoying motherhood and socialising with other parents. In order to have some income I advertised for lodgers, which were not difficult to find. It was also some security as I was not happy living in the house alone. I kept busy gardening and maintaining the house. I was also establishing some good friends. I had plenty time to devote to my daughter. She knew the alphabet when she was two years old even though she did not have much conversation. I began to realise how important formative years are in a child's life.

When Andrew's project finished he returned to London. He had no place to stay and it was not long before he won back my affection. It is difficult when there is a child involved to sever ties with a partner and I was always full of hope. My family was not aware of the situation and I would have tolerated anything just to avoid having to tell them that there were problems in our relationship. For a short time it worked but he was adamant that he wanted to go back to Australia. I did not want to do this as I was afraid that if the relationship did not work out, I would have difficulty getting back into the housing market. I was afraid of being deprived of my independence and feared commitment. I still harboured the genetic pull to my homeland: the longer that I was away from Ireland, the more patriotic I became, more so since I had my daughter.

There was a time when Andrew expressed a wish to live in Ireland as he had been there on holiday and liked it. At one stage his company was discussing doing some work there. I was ambivalent as I had been away for so long and was out of touch with the ways of rural living and my rather dysfunctional family. I did not realise at the time that all Irish families were not like mine and was often surprised when my friends would go home to their mother if they had any problems. That was the last place I would go, my first concern was that she would hear of any of my difficulties. The contract did not materialise and I was relieved: London was near enough to visit home but far away enough to lead a private life.

Men do not always like independent women; it does not suit their egos. I was in a position to call the shots which was great for me. To his friends and colleagues the property was "ours"; when the bills came they were "mine". There was a big boom in property shortly after I purchased my house. I had done very well financially. It so happened that it was good timing; the property boom had not been predicted. I was very proud of my achievements and my entrepreneurialism was beginning to make its presence felt.

Andrew bought his own property near his work and we spent weekends together, probably just for the sake of Andrea. He made a decision to go back to Australia and it was devastating. Of course telling my mother was the first thing that came to my mind. I had made many friends and kept myself busy as there was always some activity for children: ballet, swimming, gymnastics. It was so embarrassing and demoralising to be a single parent as at the time, there was a lot of negative publicity about single parents. My pride was severely dented; mainly because it was a relationship which was never intended. He was not in a good place when I met him and, as always, there is a good woman behind every man which was definitely true in my case.

This break-up was more devastating because of a child being involved. There was a lot of bitterness on my part and matters did become acrimonious. This did not affect the access times to Andrea, which I always encouraged. I can understand why parents do loose contact with their siblings if there is animosity between parents. In retrospect everything worked out well for Andrea. The fact that I had a good relationship with his mother was very beneficial, as she was always very fair and expressed her honest opinion. My daughter was three at the time and was upset initially. As he had not been living with us full-time, she got used to his absence. When he was saying farewell to her she was crying and I said, "let's sit down and cry together", which appeared to help her and she remembered it for many years. In retrospect I handled the situation in a very diplomatic manner and she did not appear to be affected psychologically. Children forget and adapt easily. There were plenty of distractions with various activities and then she started going to nursery. She always had other children over to play and she never knew what it was to be an only child. Her father and his family were in contact by letter and phone and her Granny continued to visit.

Previously when a relationship ended my first instinct was to pack my bags and go to a new environment. My daughter was what anchored me and I would not have changed this for anything. Little did I know at this time the devastation that I would have to deal with later, in the search for love and companionship.

I had a desire to go back to work but I did not have the strength to leave Andrea with anybody. She was so accustomed to having me with her all the time. I was also worried about my ability to cope with my role as a nurse, due to my own emotional issues. My profession and colleagues had always provided distraction from these. I had drifted away from Irish circles and found that comfortable, as I thought that all Irish people were like my family. Social life was centred on more cosmopolitan activities, such as theatre and concerts. Henley Regatta was one of the summer highlights. There were also open-air concerts in Regents Park, Hampstead Heath and in most of the parks in London. My daughter's Granny from Australia visited every other summer for her birthday, which was always so comforting and exciting. There were plenty of Irish artists touring the UK and plenty of traditional Irish music in the pubs and theatres. I was always proud of my heritage and enjoyed the very rich culture. I was eager to learn more about it.

When my relationship broke up I had to establish a new social circle. I did not know too many people apart from mothers and children as I had never been in that position before. I was completely lost and I started to go out on my own to the theatre and concerts. This was easy in London as there were always activities and it was acceptable to go out unaccompanied. I had no difficulty getting babysitters and could go to matinees in the theatres. There was a theatre in my area which hosted many Irish plays, which I really enjoyed. One Irish play which I attended called *Red Roses and Petrol*, I found very disturbing. It contained family conflict and raised voices which really upset me. It reminded me of my own childhood. It was becoming clear that I had, more often than not, chosen the wrong type of partner: men who would not raise their voices or tell me off. Passive aggression and lack of communication does not solve problems and they remain unresolved. Resentment festers as a result. My friend could not understand why I was so visibly affected by the play.

I remember going to see the Chieftains and Van Morrison in the Royal Albert Hall and I was hoping it would never end. Security is normally very tight at concerts; not on this occasion as people were dancing in the aisles which the band encouraged. There was a big annual Irish Fleadh Cheoil in the area where I lived, which I attended. To my surprise Joe Dolan was performing. I had seen him many times during my dancing days in the sixties, but had not known that he was still performing. He was wearing a white suit and tripped over and fell on stage, which really amused me. As I looked around I saw a man who looked like my father playing a tin whistle and became very emotional. Memories started flooding back.

Even though my situation appeared dismal, I was in a good financial position and could afford to partake of various social and recreational activities. I was walking up the road one day and was talking to an Irish lady. When we came to my house she said to me, "are you working in there?" I replied, "no, I own it", which came as a big surprise to her. There were a lot of Irish people in the area who worked mostly on the buildings and many women did not work outside the home; others did part-time work to fit in with family life.

My fear of being alone for Christmas was causing me some anxiety. It was 1989. I had a friend, Bina, from my travelling days who lived in Nova Scotia. This was the month of June and Air Canada were advertising cheap flights. I decided to take advantage of this. Going home was not an option as I had not informed them of the break-up of my relationship with Andrew. Keeping up the happy image would be difficult and anyway, my daughter would tell the story. We had a good time with Bina and her friendship was the perfect tonic at a time of great emotional turmoil. She had children and the atmosphere was very family-orientated; which provided some distraction and gave me a break. We went on a sleigh ride and the children were snow-skiing, which was very exciting for them. It was lovely to drive around to see all the Christmas decorations outside all the houses; an amazing sight against the backdrop of snow!

One day I went for a walk. It was so cold that my feet felt numb. I went to the nearest café, had a hot drink and quickly returned home. I got an idea of what hypothermia was like; my wardrobe was not suitable for this climate. Locals never saw the grass from October to April, as there was constant snowfall. People adapted to this and most were keen on winter sports.

I was financially secure and did not have to seek state assistance, which was some relief. I decided to join a single parents group. I had no experience of this socio economic group of people and found it hard to interact and be part of that scene initially. As I was living in a very sought after area and wore expensive clothes other women were often suspicious of me. I also owned my own car and was often expected to provide free taxi rides. There were family day outings arranged to the seaside and the zoo, which were very enjoyable. Andrea went to nursery school and was becoming less dependent on me. Leaving her at the nursery school is a day which I will not forget; she had been my constant companion and I was alone again. I had to put on a brave face to share her excitement. She always adapted well to every situation and made friends easily, which made life easy for me. I did some reciprocal child-minding with other mothers, which made it possible for me to go back to work.

I went home to Ireland regularly. Andrea really did enjoy all the farm animals and had fun playing with the dog and riding the donkey. She always brought a present for the dog. My brother took her out on the tractor and she was very happy with all the attention she was getting. She was the youngest child in the family and this was a great novelty. My father was always delighted when we visited. This did cause some jealousy with some of the other grandchildren. Even though my mother was very unpleasant to me, she had great praise for my daughter and was very complimentary about her good behaviour. When I returned to London I was always a nervous wreck, but lived in hope that her attitude would change. The atmosphere in the home was sitting on a volcano: you never knew when an eruption would occur. Being different from the rest of the siblings, I often found the situation intolerable. My accent, attitude, lifestyle and independence were so different to theirs.

When I returned to London after one such holiday, a friend put me in touch with a homeopath. It was the first time I had ever spoken about personal issues. More importantly, it was the first time I felt free to talk about myself and the burden started to lighten; being a nurse it was assumed that you could deal with personal problems. I was always so immersed in other people's issues that I did not focus on my own. She gave me a remedy and I went home. I could not stop working on the house and the garden. I did more work in one day than I had done for several weeks. I wrote to my mother to say how her attitude had affected me; she phoned me to discuss it. She stated that she had treated me like all the others and did not accept any blame. I decided to explore my issues further and went to a counsellor. I had enough knowledge to understand how the process worked, but found it difficult to form a therapeutic relationship with a counsellor. After a few sessions I decided not to pursue it any further. She was disappointed with my decision and concerned about my welfare.

I was regaining my confidence and felt it was time to go back to work to provide some distractions from my situation. I joined an agency and was offered a position as a district nurse, which I declined as I thought it would be too isolating. I was sent to work in different hospitals, one being the hospital where I trained. Working in different hospitals all the time did not turn out too well as I never got to know anybody. I was also missing the job satisfaction, continuity of care and also the respect and appreciation that I had had from the patients working as a full-time nurse. I was always referred to as the agency nurse, not given a name and given less attractive duties.

I decided, after all, to try district nursing and to my surprise I really loved it. The hours were suitable, working 9am to 1pm, which suited my situation. I was living in the area so travelling time would not be too great. Working in a new field of nursing was not difficult for me as I had so much experience, not just in different fields but also in different countries. I adapted well and it was a welcome boost to a very deflated morale. I always enjoyed a challenge. My manager offered me a position and was anxious for me to join the permanent staff.

An interview was arranged to formalise my working conditions. I was anxious and concerned as to whether I would be able to cope with the commitment of work. I went for the interview and was deliberately negative. I asked all the questions an employer does not want to hear - i.e. will I get holidays when I need them? My manager reassured me that I would be accommodated as much as possible. I waited a few days and decided to accept the position, which turned out to be a good one.

Resuming My Career

I was lucky to get back to work at this time as it was becoming more difficult to find jobs. Also the training programme had changed and all nurses had to have degrees. Interviews were also difficult; my clinical performance was always good but confidence was sadly lacking when it came to interviews. A new education programme was introduced and all trained staff had to have clinical updates before they could register. Andrea started going to school in September 1989. I would drop her off to a friend who would take her to school and I would pick her up in the afternoon.

One memory I have of this time was that I never had the strength to wean her off the bottle. Even though the school was within walking distance I drove there and took a bottle. She lay down in the back of the car so that her friends would not see her enjoy her treat. That memory has stayed with both of us. She was a quiet, shy child who the teachers said loved a lot of praise. She did not interact well in class with teachers. One teacher thought that she may be deaf; when it was discovered that shyness was the main cause of her problems, the teacher took her in hand and she progressed favourably.

One day she played a trick on her friend by going under the desk and tickling her feet. The friend let a roar thinking it was a mouse. Instead of telling her off the teacher brought her up and cuddled her. I can imagine how upset she was at having been caught out. She had a great sense of fun from an early age. (There may be some hereditary factors at play). One day she came home from school very upset. She said that another child kept telling her that she did not like her. I advised her to walk away and ignore her, she did that. A few days later the child came to her said that she was sorry and did like her. Wearing glasses and having the surname that sounded like a fast food restaurant meant that she got teased a lot; but she rose above this and turned it into a joke. There was no recognition of bullying at this time.

She became very popular at school with both boys and girls and had difficulty choosing who to invite to her birthday parties. Her parties were a great event and I made every effort to make a cake with the latest theme and decorations. Her granny from Australia came over every other year to celebrate.

My work was very rewarding and interesting. I really enjoyed my role as a district nurse. It was very varied and we had to deal with all kinds of situations: liaising with GPs, social workers, palliative care, hospitals and many other organisations. We had a lot of in-service training and study pertinent to our role, which kept me stimulated. I was working in a very socially deprived area with many people living in poor circumstances: they had many social issues, were lonely and suffered poor health. The only contact some would have was a visit from the district nurse or social services. It was a very multi-cultural area and my travelling experience was a great asset. I was open to their often different customs. Initially I thought that I would not be able to deal with the poor conditions in which they lived.

Many of the staff had been in the same job for years and as the service was developing, they were not too happy with the increased work load. They were not accustomed to change. When I got to know the people and saw how appreciative they were, I ignored the sometimes appalling living conditions. I came away with a feeling of satisfaction that I was in a position to bring some happiness into their sad lives. As I was the most junior member of staff I was often given less attractive duties; but I turned this into a challenge and enjoyed the appreciation from the clients.

There was great interaction between the different services and it was not at all isolated, as I had previously thought. Working in the community a different relationship exists to that in a hospital: the patients are in their own homes and you also get to know their families. They are hospitable and make the nurse very welcome. One Indian man I visited used to say the three best things in life are Irish girls, Kerrygold butter and Guinness! More time can be spent with the patients as there is less distraction. As a district nurse I was eligible to have a company car. This was terrific as my car was becoming unreliable and I could not afford to update it. The Health Authority was responsible for the maintenance of the car and I received a mileage allowance for petrol.

My career was satisfying and I was coping well. I was still searching for answers about my personal life and relationships. The Health Authority set up a Psychological service for staff, which I decided to avail of. I made an appointment and was seen by a psychologist. Following a detailed assessment of my childhood he said it was obvious that there was some buried trauma. He did not think it sufficiently urgent to investigate it at this time since there was waiting lists. He said that it was typical Irish story, big families, not being listened to and unhappy marriages. Research has shown that of all the ethnic groups, Irish people were most in need of psychological and psychiatric care. It later emerged that 35% to 45% of those who were sexually and emotionally abused in the care system and by the church, emigrated to the UK.

I enjoyed all the child-rearing activities and enrolled Andrea in ballet, gymnastics, music, drama and swimming. It was 1990. I was hoping that she would do Irish dancing and the things which I never had the opportunity to do; but to my disappointment she was not interested. We had a drop-in centre and plenty of activities were laid on by the council for children. We became friendly with a couple who had one child and we went on trips together. They were involved in a charity and had access to a Longboat. Being a Piscean I had always loved water activities. When the boat was available we hired it to go on trips on the river Thames and overnight trips to the surrounding areas. It was fantastic to see London while cruising along the Thames at our own speed. We went camping and took trips to Butlins holiday camp which was on the coast; I had never thought of going on holiday to Butlins but to my amazement it was terrific. It was so child-orientated; they produced all the children's plays which I had never seen. I was living the childhood I never had. Audience participation was encouraged and I enjoyed seeing the children having so much fun. Andrea thought holidays were only Butlins and when we came to Ireland she asked 'where were all the rides?' We went there several times as there were special offers on at different times of the year. At first we went self-catering but due to lack of adult company at night time, it proved to be too lonely. I booked full board accommodation, which was more satisfactory as I met other people in similar circumstances. There were organised activities for the children and it gave me a break to pursue some of my own activities.

In rural Ireland there were not many activities for children but I remember my father taking us to variety shows in our local parish, which we would reproduce at home. My father being a musician meant that there was always plenty of entertainment at home during my childhood. At this time in London I became a member of the Youth Hostel Association and we went on weekend trips to different areas around the South East and Wales. I met up with many interesting people and Andrea always made good friends. Frequently we stayed with friends in Manchester during the half-term breaks. There were always activities during the week but it was lonely at the weekends, so it was necessary to plan other activities.

It was amazing, the simple things that are amusing to children. One day we went to the park with a few parents and children. We did not hear the park keeper announcing that the park was going to be closed, so we got locked in. We did not know what to do and rang the police. They were not too happy as my friend dialled 999. Nevertheless they had to get us out. It was so funny being lifted over big gates with bicycles, bags and other children's toys. To the children it was an exciting adventure and they talked about it long afterwards.

I went home twice a year, usually at Easter and summer. It might sound strange but I had comfort and security from being with my family and my daughter loved the country life. She loved mucking around the yard and playing with insects and animals. She was enjoying the same things that I enjoyed as a child. My mother liked her and always said what a mannerly child she was. At the same time, with the arrival of my daughter I was no longer in a position to be providing financial support. Having travelled from London in a car with a small child was no easy task and I needed some nurturing. I was often very hurt but tried to ignore this and concentrate on the positive aspects of my life. Professionally all was going well and my daughter was well adjusted and happy. She had always wanted a cat so we went to RSPCA where we got a lovely cat. When we went on holiday she could not wait to get back to see the cat and had fun dressing her up in dolls clothes and teaching her tricks.

I missed not having a partner and somebody to spend time with when Andrea went to bed. I went to shows in the West End and sometimes to matinees. I had a reasonable social life mainly centred on matters relating to parenting and my daughter. My friends came to visit. During half-term I booked a holiday to go to Majorca to get away for a break, hoping to meet new people, particularly of the opposite sex in similar circumstances. Andrea met a friend on the plane and spent most of the time playing with her so I was on my own quite a lot. I had never been on a package holiday before and did not like all the commercialism of where we were staying. We decided to go freelance and explore the island on local transport. We went up to the north of the island, to Alcudia, which was a real adventure as the road went through large mountains. Looking out the window of the bus was a bit eerie as the road was very windy and there was an enormous drop. This added to the excitement of the trip. Andrea really enjoyed the adventure and felt very grown up.

The holiday provided some distraction for a short period and I returned to work, which was my security blanket. My self-esteem remained low and I did not like being alone. One day we went swimming in a place where there were mirrors all around. I got a glimpse of a person in the mirror and thought she looks nice. On further inspection I realised it was me. It made me see that I did not look as bad as I felt! I thought nobody would ever love me or that I could never love again. I was devoid of emotion.

A Snake in the Grass

Friends of mine had joined a dating agency and I thought that this was a good idea. I was always very careful and selective about partners. The agency assessed people and tried to match them. I was the voice of reason to many of my friends as I had so much life experience. I just wanted a companion to go to movies and theatre with no commitment; I had no desire to cohabit and did not want any complications. I was very cynical about love and relationships. Unless they were financially secure and had no baggage, I would dismiss them swiftly. I got a phone call from a very nice Irishman named Frank and thought that, as I did not have any luck with other nationalities, it was time to get back to my own culture.

I arranged to meet him and had great trust in him as he was Irish. I thought that at last I had met Mr Right; I was very excited and thought, "this is it!" He was not good looking but compensated with very intelligent conversation, great finesse and by wearing designer clothes. He told me that he was a captain of a ship in the Middle East. Initially he was very generous; he was pulling out all the stops just to impress me. In retrospect I suppose I would have believed anything at the time: my endorphins were flowing, which clouded my rational thinking. Frank had also left Ireland at a young age and was very cosmopolitan, which I admired; we had lots to talk about

He was very critical about Ireland and the narrow-mindedness that existed there. With the experience of my dysfunctional family and Irish customs I guess this was music to my ears, as it sounded so familiar. I had not dated Irishmen or moved in Irish circles for years and Irish family life was never discussed. Most other nationalities would have difficulty understanding how Irish life was in the 50's and 60's and I spent my life concealing this. I guess I was so excited because I felt that I had met somebody who understood me.

The story about to enfold is very disturbing and I can only give some of the details; my encounter with Frank would be a book in itself. A friend, who heard the whole story, said afterwards that he must have got his tips from seeing the movie *Sleeping with the Enemy*. It emerged that he was a cunning, plausible psychopath who preyed on vulnerable women and it turned out that his credentials were rather unsavoury. When a person is vulnerable there is always somebody lurking in the long grass to take advantage. He established what my tastes and plans were and surprisingly it always appeared to coincide with his expectations. He said that he was involved in some kind of intelligence, which would appear to be true; he was very skilful in extracting information from people. When I expressed an interest in returning to Ireland he said that he had the same thing in mind. He would buy the best glossy magazines with big mansions with stud farms for sale in Ireland. He proposed to me and said that he would retire just to be with me. Being the perfect gentleman he gave me the privilege of picking properties of my choice; at the time I did not realise that I would be paying. He said that he was a millionaire and wanted to own horses and have a stud farm: obviously having established my liking for country life and horses.

I was telling my friend, Ann, about my new partner as we were walking through Richmond Park. She said that fraudsters do not come dressed in rags. I thought that she was jealous and dismissed her opinion. He kept saying that "you and the child will never want for anything." He said that he would refurbish my house to increase the value prior to selling it. Before I met him I was doing well and had planned to move to a bigger house in a very sought after area. He also wanted me to leave work. He would leave my house dressed in his Captain's uniform and say he was going to work. It later emerged that he would go to his mother's place, or another girlfriend's place and spend time there, then return a few days later saying that he had been at sea. He kept in contact by mobile phone, which was relatively new at the time, so there was no way of knowing where he was. During his visits, if he wanted to get away he would get a friend to phone him and say that there was some emergency at work. He had family who colluded with him also. He spoke other languages which I couldn't understand, and I did not know what plans he was making.

I went to Ireland and when I returned he said that he had left his job to spend more time with me. He had moved all his property into my house; in fact he had moved all my clothes just to make space for his own elaborate wardrobe. I had given him a key to keep an eye on the place. I was shocked and felt overpowered and was afraid to raise any objections. We never discussed living together. He wanted me to book exotic holidays by my credit card and he would pay me later. He started up a building business. On one occasion I went to visit my friend in Manchester and when I returned he had started knocking down walls in my house.

There was some damp in one room but he invented a list of all the faults which needed to be addressed. His alleged plan was to go into property development. He spoke with a great air of authority and was very confident. He convinced people that he was very affluent. He said that I was not to worry; he would take care of all financially. My lovely home had become a building site; he wanted me to go and live in a hotel while work was going on. Luckily I did not fall for this as I would be lumbered with the bill. He did unnecessary work and chipped the walls back to the brick. Some days there were ten or twelve people working there. He built on a new extension at the back which had no planning permission: a fact which I did not know until much later

There were men coming looking for work which fed into his grandiosity. Initially he paid up front with my money and established a good credit rating and then opened accounts with various building suppliers. He did have a brother and sister who ran or worked in a building business outside London. He ran up a big bill with the agency and nobody got paid. He sold off furniture and anything that he could get money for and said that it he would replace it with much better quality. Then he said that he was having difficulty getting money transferred and asked me to get a loan until it arrived. I had almost paid off my mortgage and had no difficulty getting finance, I also had some savings and stocks and shares.

He phoned me one day at work and said not to return to the house unless I had £10,000 just to tide him over until he got his money transferred from overseas. I had a good credit rating as a home owner with secure employment and it was easy to get a loan. He was aware of my assets as it appears he had looked at all my financial statements. I was walking round in a daze and trying to keep a brave face in front of the neighbours, friends, my daughter and colleagues. I was hopeful and did half-believe that he would honour his promise and tried to stay on good terms with him. He then said that he had cancer and all his wealth would be mine, just to get sympathy and attention. He was very paranoid and thought people were out to get him; which may well have been true. He put security alarms in my house. It now appears that he had other women in the same boat, as I often found that some of my good clothes were missing. He would bring me gifts which I know were stolen from them. He would steal my cheque book and forge my signature and take my bank and credit card and use them without my knowledge. The bank was sending me letters about my overdrawn account, which he intercepted and kept from me. Eventually I went to the bank and discovered what he had been doing. He just literally wrecked my house and then I had to try to get it back to habitable state. I was a nervous wreck and had lost an enormous amount of weight, was not sleeping and looked as pale as a ghost, wondering how I was going to cope.

I asked him to leave my house and he refused. He was going out drinking and coming home late and intimidating me. Andrea was becoming upset as he was reprimanding her and not allowing her to watch her videos or TV programmes. I tried to keep out of his way and was away from the house as much as possible. Eventually I went to the police and explained my dilemma and they said that I should leave the house. I explained that it was my property but they said that it did not matter. There was no awareness or support for people who were involved in any domestic disturbances. At this time the police were loath to interfere, since it was hard to get a conviction when women would refuse to pursue the complaint, resulting in wasting police time. Currently the police in Britain have been given new powers to enter the home of alleged domestic abusers and promptly remove the accused; too often it had been the victim who had to flee the home. Frank was so plausible that it was hard to decipher if he was telling the truth or lies: he was a pathological liar. My distraction was to go to the park to meet with other parents, and friends. One day when I returned home, to my great delight, he was not there.

Andrea went to bed as she was exhausted. I went out to my back garden. A man's voice from the end of the garden called me over but he did not identify himself initially. He asked me who was in the house and I replied just me and my daughter. He then explained that he was police, demanded the keys of my house and that I go to the police station. I refused to do this as Andrea was asleep. He was very curt and intimidating. He told me to get her up and proceed as instructed to the police station. I then asked him if I could take my own car. He said, "If you get into your car I will arrest you." I did not know what was going on and was not enlightened by the policeman. It probably hit me that it was something to do with Frank, as there was no other reason why I should be spoken to in such a manner by the police. I left my house and walked down to the station, very embarrassed to be supervised by the police. I was talking to my daughter as if nothing was wrong. When I went there I was not offered the services of a solicitor and my handbag was taken and searched. I felt like a criminal and had never been a situation like this. A policewoman took my six year old daughter away and tried to extract information from her.

After taking a detailed statement I was allowed to return home, not knowing what was going on. It also appears that my car and home were searched without a search warrant. I later heard from neighbours that the road was blocked and nobody was allowed access to their homes. It transpired that this man had been involved in a hold up at a petrol station with an imitation gun; his car number was linked to my address. He was nowhere to be found and returned a few days later not giving any information about his whereabouts. I cannot remember all the details but when the police found him there was a warrant out for his arrest for drunken driving, he was taken to court but I do not know the outcome. He told the police that he had information about IRA activities and of course it was music to their ears: there was a great fear of bombs and other political unrest. They believed him and thought that he would be a great asset with their intelligence gathering. He got away with a lot of bad behaviour. He was also very funny and kept the police extremely amused. Amongst other things he told them that he had invested a lot of money in my house. They had great sympathy for him as he was so convincing.

One day he complained of having chest pain and an ambulance was called. He was taken to hospital. He was on first name terms with the police and one female officer said that some women are never pleased, as she believed his story. It was his way of seeking attention to get some sympathy. When he was discharged I refused to let him back into the house. He already had a key and got back in when I was at work. Secretly I always thought that he would honour his promise and pay me back the money. I was living in fear, not knowing what he was going to do next. There were several arguments and I was continually asking him to leave but he refused. Going through the courts takes several months and, as he was claiming to have invested so much money in my house, it would be a difficult struggle to have him evicted. One day there was a minor altercation resulting in me having bruises on my arm. I capitalised on this and went to the police. They came and took him away. When I informed my solicitor he said that it was a stroke of genius to get him out so easily in the end.

He harassed, embarrassed and intimidated me. He rang my family telling them that I was in involved in political activities. He rang my manager and told her that I was claiming benefits; which was not true. He stole my work diary from my car, which I had to report as it was feared that he would contact any of the clients. He sent taxis and estate agents around on false pretences. He put ads in the local paper alleging that I was selling property belonging to him. There were building materials left behind which he claimed were his. Consequently I was kept busy answering the phone. He got his own friends to ring to confirm that those items were for sale. He did everything to discredit me and portray me as a bad person to the court. It did not work!

He found out my solicitor's name and rang her, posing as his solicitor and got information regarding the case. He was very articulate and knowledgeable, he even fooled my solicitor. He continually phoned my friends and work place, telling lies in an attempt to isolate me so that I would not have support. My solicitor, who dealt with family law, refused to take the case any further as she thought that I was giving him information. My regular solicitor, who was executor of my will, came to my house one day saying that a man had contacted him to say that I had died. Being the executor of my will he had to follow up on the call and offered his services to represent me, which did not turn out to be the most satisfactory of arrangements.

My solicitor advised me to send Andrea to Australia to her father and suggested that I go to a women's refuge. I told him that I had no intention of doing either and that he had to work with me and my daughter staying where we were. I was advised by this solicitor that I was not entitled to legal aid, which was not correct, and he said that I should work full-time. He said that he had contacts where I could get full-time work in an old people's home. This would mean that I would also lose my company car, which I did not want to do. I also loved my position as a district nurse and the part-time hours suited me. I was not in any fit state to cope with full-time work. When my barrister was employed she said that of course I would qualify for legal aid. Even though I was very distressed, I had the strength to make logical decisions and do what was practical for me.

Work on the house had come to a standstill as I did not have any more money. Builders merchants were coming looking for him as apparently he had run up accounts with them, several of the builders were not paid either. Employees who had worked for several days were not paid; they were coming looking for work and also to collect their outstanding pay. The contact address he gave was the street number of the Police Station; which in retrospect was amusing! They were inundated with mail addressed to him, nobody could track him down. Ubiquitous would be the appropriate way to describe him. When they did manage to track him down he always came up with the excuse that there was some hold up with the foreign exchange. Nobody knew that I had been in a relationship with him, so he was also telling them that the client (me) had not paid him.

One merchant said that he was going to take away some doors and other items which had not been paid for, but I pleaded with them and they said that they would pursue him. I was not aware at the time that he had my phone tapped; he could monitor my activities and conversations. My phone was a great source of comfort as my friends were constantly in touch for support. He was intimidating my friends and my daughter and I was terrified of what was going to happen. I now realised that this man was mentally ill and a psychopath. Andrea's father came to visit and Frank sprayed paint stripper on his company car, even though he had parked it well away from my house.

He also sprayed paint stripper on another of my friend's cars. He watched every move I made and knew who visited. He wanted to isolate me from any support, which luckily he was not successful in doing. At the time there were no laws or support to protect women against domestic violence, nor were there laws against harassment or fraudulent activities in domestic situations. I was determined not to leave my home as I knew exactly what he had in mind. If I left he would take possession of my property and leave me homeless. At that time I would prefer to die than be destitute. I lived in fear of the postman coming, not knowing what surprise was in store for me. One day, to my great surprise, I received a letter with a cheque for one thousand pounds which I had won as a result of purchasing a ticket to support St Martin De Porres. I jumped with joy. Once again my strong faith had not let me down.

Some of my friends feared for my safety and were getting impatient with me, as they thought that I should go to a women's refuge. He told me that everybody had a breaking point; sadly for him he did not find mine. One day he called the police to say that somebody was going to throw acid in my face and they came and spent some time to protect me. I knew that this was intimidation as he wanted to disrupt the planning for Andrea's Holy Communion celebrations. He told the police that I had drugs hidden in the attic and police came with a search warrant but, of course, none were found. I complained to the police about this, they said that they were legally bound to investigate all complaints. I had become immune to his tactics and was not afraid. Even though I had got an injunction, he breached the conditions many times, by getting other people to do his dirty work. One day I went to work and when I came out from the office my company car was stolen; I knew who was responsible but could not say so. One of the staff drove me home as I was too distressed to work. Frank had taken the second key from my house. He phoned me later to see if everything was alright: I did not even mention the car being stolen. I had to do my duty on foot until another car could be provided.

He paid nocturnal visits to vandalise my property and write nasty slogans on my walls. I was given another car and he came and removed the number plates. He set a fire in my garden and the fire brigade had to be called. The incidents would be followed by a phone call from him to say that he would protect me if I let him back. I had my telephone number changed several times, but he always managed to get the current one by some devious means. He continually watched me and would ring my home at all hours of the night. He phoned the Inland Revenue to say that I was not declaring my full income. Following an assessment by Revenue a settlement was agreed. I did not owe much as the income from lodgers only brought an income slightly above my liability for tax. Nevertheless it was a very distressing experience.

One day he was found outside my house with a gun, which later proved to be a fake one. He was picked up by the police who gave me an emergency alarm. I had to change my bank account details; locks on the doors also had to be changed. I had to re-mortgage my house and borrow money from other people; which included having to get child maintenance upfront. Frank had taken details of my mortgage and phoned the bank to say that he was going to pay off my mortgage, fortunately they were aware of the situation.

I was trying to keep all this from my family as their judgmental attitude would be difficult to deal with. Now that this had happened it had to be dealt with, and hindsight is a great thing. Looking back, I just do not know how I kept going. There were several court cases but each time he sent a doctor's sick note at the last minute so the case had to be rescheduled. I had to live with the fear of him being at liberty to harass me. I had to call the police so many times that the superintendent suggested that I was doing it just to have the police coming around. By the time they arrived he would be nowhere to be found. I was not happy with how my solicitor was presenting my case to the court. I did not know anything about the law and it came as a surprise to me that I had to present my case to the solicitor. The solicitor then employed a barrister to present the case to the judge. Many times information got lost in translation or was misinterpreted. During one court hearing the judge did not find the harassment breaches sufficiently serious to sentence him. I broke down in tears and when the judge saw this he asked me to testify. I do not know how I got the courage to stand up in court and explain my dilemma. It was only then that I got some satisfaction.

My position as a district nurse in the local area was a fairly prestigious and well respected. The judge treated me with great respect and at last I established some credibility. The breaches of the injunction were many but he kept up the harassment. I wrote a letter to the Police Complaints Authority, expressing my fears and also the fact that my tormenter was allowed to get away with such actions. The Police Superintendent came to my house to discuss the matter and explain their difficulty in tracking him down. It was very difficult to serve him with injunction papers as he had so many different aliases. I wrote a letter to my solicitor stating what information I wanted to be presented to the judge. I highlighted the fears and distress which I was experiencing.

Finally Frank moved to a new address in 1993. He was burgled and had to call the police. When they arrived they realised that he was on their wanted list for other matters and arrested him. He was given a free holiday, courtesy of her Majesty the Queen, in Wormwood Scrubs prison, but it appears he had some influential friends and got out after a short period. His mother lived in a council house not too far away, which was where he went for refuge.

The harassment went on for five years. I never felt completely free of him until I left the UK in 1997. My friends and work colleagues were so fantastic to me that it helped me to cope with his behaviour, which was very frightening. When my mother was admitted to hospital in Ireland he managed to get the number of the hospital and phoned her. He posed as my priest, telling her that my partner had cancer but that he was going to leave me very well off. I managed to get my fare home, using my credit card which was stretched to the limit, but he had found the ticket in my car, which he stole and presented himself at the airport to harass me. I ignored him! He also found out what I was wearing and phoned customs to check me. When I got to customs they pulled me aside to search my luggage. It occurred to me what he had done and when I explained they understood and there were no further questions. I tried to keep it from my family and was a nervous wreck. I had the responsibility of protecting my daughter from the entire disturbance. The police described him as a Walter Mitty character.

I went to a priest hoping that he would give me some 'divine guidance'; but unfortunately all he suggested was that I go to counselling. I was disappointed as I was expecting that he would use some 'divine intervention' to get this undesirable man out of my life. But I suppose I did get the strength and courage to bear my burden. I had not been sleeping and had to cope with working and getting my property back to habitable condition. One Sunday I went to church and the homily was about Greed. The priest said that you can make a big effort to save and be very careful about money only to lose it to some con artist. My first instinct was to stand up and shout: "Are yis talking to me?"

I was really exhausted due to lack of sleep and worry. I went to my GP to get sleeping tablets. He gave me some with reluctance and said that this was only a temporary solution. He referred me for counselling. I was seen promptly as I had been placed on a waiting list previously. My counsellor was very concerned about me and requested that I give up my sleeping tablets, fearing that I was going to take an overdose. He did not have any need to worry as I had a big challenge on my hands and a great battle to fight! Counselling did provide some support and comfort but it did not appear to address the fundamental issues. My counsellor was not of western culture and did not establish that my relationship with my mother was having such a detrimental effect on my life. What is acceptable in one culture is not acceptable in another.

I still carried on with life and had great support from friends and work colleagues; not that they had known the details in full. The whole experience was a great learning curve, embarrassing and frightening as it was. Research carried out at the University of Colorado's Business school by Professor Vinit Desai concluded that failure is a terrific teacher. His team found in their research that "knowledge gained from success was often fleeting while knowledge gained from failure stuck around for years." Failure is much more valuable than success. More can be learned from failure and one can gain insight into where you went wrong.

It is hard to believe what anybody could learn from an experience like this but I learned a lot. Firstly I never had the confidence to speak to an audience, but I did this in court. I learned a lot about the law and looking back, I was instrumental in getting the court to see how much distress I was suffering. I learned how much my colleagues had appreciated me and my work ethic. I also learned how to manage money, as there were times when I thought that I would have to sell my property to pay off my debts. I also learned who my friends were and who stood by me at this distressing time. There were people who could have helped but did not. My solicitor asked if I had any family who could help but the rejection would have hurt too much. I would not even ask. By this time I was becoming immune to hassle and no matter what happened, I was thinking that it could be worse. I was always full of positivity and hope: having to fight my corner as a child instilled great strength in me.

Following Frank's imprisonment he did leave me alone physically and even though I was living in fear, I started to get some normality back into my life. I got some new lodgers. He often phoned them to tell them that their life was in danger and to get out, but they ignored this. The income was helpful plus I had somebody in the house for support. I usually recruited from local colleges or on the local newspaper. I rarely had a vacancy as good quality accommodation was in short supply; my terms and conditions were very good.

I had many lodgers from all over the world and it was a very successful venture. One lodger I had was a refugee from Afghanistan, Muhammed. He had been a medic in the Mujahedeen army and had very interesting stories to tell. He always wore a cap as he had a bad injury sustained during the war. Although he was going to the local college he was not westernised. He had never mixed with women and was a strict Muslim. He appreciated the comfortable accommodation and my assistance in helping him to assimilate into western society. He was happy to talk about his life, which I found quite fascinating. He also helped me to do some decorating and get my home back in order. Also his rent enabled me to replace the property which had been lost.

He was very capable and as my patients were often looking for handymen to do odd jobs, I was happy to recommend him. They were very pleased with him, as he was so honest and reliable. On his side, he was very pleased with the extra income and about getting to know the western ways. He stayed with me for three years and kept in touch by phone for some time. He had watched the Eurovision Song contest in 1994 when *Riverdance* was first performed and called me to say how much he had enjoyed it.

The Parting Glass

My mother had been looking after my father at home as he was having mini-strokes from 1984 until his death in 1992. He was always easy to please so that did not prove too difficult. There was plenty of help around and there were adequate health services. Of course everybody had to follow my mother's instructions and even when I went home, she had to tell me how to perform nursing tasks. Not doing exactly what she said did not go down too well. One day he asked me for a kiss, I was overwhelmed with emotion. I felt so sorry for him that he had been denied the pleasure of any expression of love from his children. Expressing love or saying anything good about my father did not please my mother. Being a parent myself this upset me greatly.

He had an episode and was semi-conscious for a few days; we were all around him and thought he was going to die. The rosary beads were all out and his breathing became very shallow; next thing he gave a kick and woke up and looked around. We were all very surprised and my sister-in-law said that he was always a practical joker. I was relieved that he did not die, as being a nurse my mother would insist that I lay him out, which I would have had difficulty doing. A local lady was a nurse and I asked her if she would do the deed, which she agreed. He improved but was still housebound: which must have been very frustrating for him, having been so much involved in the local social life through his music. He had plenty of visitors and always loved to see his family coming. He was very fond of my daughter but he could never pronounce her name. In addition to sharing the same birthday, she has also inherited his musical ability.

Soon after my mother became ill due to self-imposed stress and had to be admitted to hospital. My father had to be admitted to a nursing home. He thought that this was a temporary arrangement and agreed to go. The nursing home was what was known down the years as the Poor House/County Home dating back to Famine times; there was a great stigma attached to being sent there. It would be unthinkable for his generation to go there. In all the years that he had passed it, driving cattle and sheep to the fair, he would never have dreamt of ending his days there. He had a great love for his land. Once he went to London on holidays and was taken to see all the sights, but when he returned home he said that he would not give up his cabbage garden for all of London. He was a very good farmer, a good judge and producer of livestock. He was very proud of his produce and interested in their progress. At the hospital he recognised that he had sold some sheep to one of the nursing attendants in the past. He asked him how had the sheep had done, the attendant thought that he was confused and dismissed his comment. Later he remembered the deal and assured him that that they had done well. His bed was near a window and there were rabbits playing outside, which he enjoyed.

My mother was in hospital for some time and no diagnosis had been reached. When she was discharged my sister Florence took in her into her home and rearranged her family schedule to accommodate her. She must have been with her for at least six months. When she returned to her own home she did not express any gratitude and said that she was pleased to back home. My sister had entertained all the family who came to visit my mother. Nothing anybody ever did would please her and my family tolerated this. My mother was very generous to my sister and her children. My parents' 50th wedding anniversary was in 1991 and was celebrated in the nursing home. My mother knew that my father would want me to be there so the celebration was arranged to coincide with my annual leave. I was surprised at the different opinions and disagreements that made even small arrangements difficult. There were disproportionate outbursts for very trivial reasons. Any arrangement or discussion usually ended up in conflict, which I found very uncomfortable.

My father had a few episodes of mini-strokes. He could have gone home for Christmas but my mother would not take him out in case he refused to go back. He died two years later in the nursing home in December 1992. On his deathbed my mother asked him if he wanted anything and he replied that he "just wanted to go home." It was a sad end to such a good family man, who had provided so well for us in such hard times. He had bought a tape recorder previously to record some of his music and my mother asked him who he wanted to leave this to: he said to me. I spent that Christmas at home, which was the first time I had done so in years. I enjoyed the security of being in my family home and I returned to work looking forward to my next holiday, which would be Easter.

Andrea always enjoyed her holidays but was always anxious to get back to her cat. When we returned home she went out to the garage to find that the cat had died. She was distraught and had to be consoled. I promised her that I would get another cat which I did. My lodger had been looking after the cat and did not want to disrupt our holiday by telling us. The cat had previously been attacked by a dog and had lost an eye and was also suffering from breathing difficulties. The weather had been cold and the cat must have got a chest infection, resulting in her death. I was exhausted and emotionally fragile due to the travelling and dealing with all the challenges back home. This was another situation which I could have done without as it needed tactful handling. My daughter wrote the following poem at eight years old:

Pepsi was a lovely cat
She used to wear a lovely hat
I used to call her funny names
Both of us used to play lovely games.
She was oh such a lovely cat
And I will miss her that is that
She loved me and I loved her back
And she used to give me a dirty rat
She was so loved she will be heard
And she gave me a lovely bird
Flapping around and then flew away
Oh the day that she died was a horrible day.

Community Nursing

I was very involved with my work and was finding it very challenging, as well as a distraction from my personal life. At the time there were great reforms in the Health Service and the Community Services were developing rapidly. Prior to 1990, the role of the community nurse was limited and involved social care. Hospital at Home Care Service was set up to allow for patients to be discharged home early, in the care of a GP and a district nurse. This was a terrific idea as it freed beds for more acute and emergency patients. Research also proved that patients recover much quicker in their own environment and they were not exposed to hospital infections. A leg ulcer clinic was set up and in-service training was provided. Prior to this patients with leg ulcers were admitted and spent several months in hospital to become institutionalized, presenting more difficulties on discharge.

Health Promotion was one of our roles and we had to go to different venues to check the health and welfare of the public. This was a very new and modern initiative in the Health Service. I was working part-time and it fitted in well with the care of my daughter. It was difficult during half-term times as it was not always possible to get time off to coincide with those holidays, or when she was sick. Sometimes I took her with me in the car during the visits; which was not exactly safe or allowed. Child-minders or schools are not anxious to have sick children, as infection spreads to other kids so easily, so I was left with little choice. Sometimes I dropped her off at the library and set her up to do some reading and painting, hoping that I would not have an accident and be unable to return to pick her up. I had some lodgers who were working different shifts and as I was working in the area, I could come home to check that all was well. There were summer schemes set up for the holidays and I availed of this. In summer we came home to Ireland on holidays, which we both really looked forward to as we both loved country life. I always enjoyed the interaction and fun my daughter had with her cousins.

My work was very interesting and gave me great satisfaction. The District Nursing qualification was very academic and it was difficult to qualify for training. I could not advance past staff nurse status without completing the training. The Sister on my team had a heart attack and somebody had to deputise in her absence. My manager asked me to act in this capacity, even though there were other people more qualified to do it. During reorganisation some senior members lost their positions and were on protected salaries. They were qualified to deputise. I was not happy with her decision as I was not fully aware of the duties of managing the team. I had been working part-time and did the clinical work. I was not familiar with management, which was a different system from the hospital setting. I discussed my apprehension with my manager and was very flattered to be told that I was the most capable, adaptable and experienced person available. I had been in leadership roles for many years in previous positions and had no difficulty managing staff. When I thought about it I was very flattered and appreciated that she had such confidence in my ability. At the time there were budgetary constraints; my manager said that she would try to get me an extra allowance for deputising in the absence of the sister. This did not concern me as I was always more motivated by job satisfaction than by financial gain.

Compliments were in short supply in my life for some time, even though my employers had stood by me during my terrible ordeal. An optimistic person by nature, I felt that this challenge was waiting for me. As the community was developing and progressing I felt confident that I would find the role very fulfilling. I had established great rapport with all the different agencies, was well complimented and appreciated by all. I took my work very seriously and often took work home to get my team organised. The GPs were pleased and complimentary about my efficiency, which was motivating me further and all targets were being met.

Even though I was working part-time I was fulfilling the role of a full-time Sister. I am by nature efficient and impatient: qualities which do not often go down well with other colleagues but it sure gets the work done. I was in my element having so much responsibility and being so appreciated. Stress for me is a very motivating factor.

The patients were so complimentary and often rang my manager to say how helpful I had been to them. They loved having some fun to distract them from their dull existence. My good sense of humour was very helpful and it was always very rewarding to put a smile on a lonely patient's face. Humour is one of the world's weapons for self-preservation. It is well known that humour, more than anything else in the human make-up, can afford an ability to rise above any situation. The area was multi-cultural and being Irish was an advantage.

It so happened that I did not have a hard act to follow as the team was not run efficiently and records were not up to date. The Sister whom I had been deputising for, Sister Smith, was a mature student who did training late in life and was more interested in the academic side. I was mainly interested in clinical work and face to face contact with patients. I was a student assessor and had been her mentor during her student days and then she became my line manager. Working with her was not easy: she had no experience and her organisational skills were sadly lacking. She was very arrogant and often upset the patients with her dictatorial manner. She was not experienced in working in a multi-cultural society and did not treat all people equally. When she returned to work she told our manager that she did not feel welcome. She was right about that as she had not been missed at all. In fact the patients thought that she had left and were surprised to see her back; which probably upset her. My manager called me in to discuss this with me and there was nothing I could say about the matter. Sister Smith did not want to admit to all the improvements and the high standard which had been established in her absence. The conflict between us grew, but as I was working out in the district most of the time I got on with my work.

Many times the patients would ring, asking for me and she would say: "I am the Sister how can I help?" I was channelling all my energies into my work and deriving a great sense of self-worth from it. We had one Indian GP who had to be dealt with in a diplomatic way. There was a complaint which had to be addressed and the sister asked me to write a letter to the GP concerned. I did this reluctantly and in a very diplomatic way but Sister Smith did not think that this was sufficient. She wrote a letter which did not meet with my approval and asked me to sign it, I refused to do so.

She was the union representative and was away on union business frequently; she also had study leave. I was leading the team most of the time anyway, without any conflict with other agencies. If there were any issues from junior staff she would always take the side of management, which upset staff. It suited her to side with management, as she was getting approved and funded for study leave and benefits of her choice.

I applied to do a further education course dealing with Aids and related illnesses. She tried to obstruct this by asking me if I was going to fund it myself. My absence would mean that she would have to take all the responsibility and do more work. We had some patients with this illness and I was eager to learn more about it; it was early 1990's and relatively new at the time. Further education relevant to our duty was encouraged. It was only a short experiential learning course through a University. I struggled with the academic side but got help with the presentation from a friend who was also going to University. I got a very good grade, which was a great boost to my deflated morale. It was very therapeutic for me also, as there was a lot of counselling and exploring of childhood and personal issues; and appropriate books were recommended

One book which was very relevant to my own life, *The Drama of Being a Child* written by Alice Miller. It emphasises the importance of a child being able to express feelings clearly and plainly, without fear or censure. The adult must be able to accommodate the child's many and various emotions: not only of joy and sorrow but also jealousy, greed, anger and so on. The losses and traumas of childhood need not lead to neurotic development if the child is given the opportunity to express grief and anger. Denial of this essential expression can lead to a wound that can never form a scar and can bleed at any time. As we increase in age, life continues to offer us a challenge. Our ability to cope with this will reflect ways in which we have integrated our earlier life experience.

Other recommended reading was a book by American author, Dr Kuebler-Ross, on *Death and Dying*, which describes the different stages of grief. My understanding was that bereavement is only when a person dies but loss can be due to separation, divorce or even the loss of a treasured pet. People grieve in different ways, depending on what they have lost. The most dangerous condition is when they become stuck, unable to reach the acceptance stage, perhaps expressing anger or going through depression many years later. It is so important at this stage to seek professional help to get assistance in rebuilding your life. When a person divorces or separates they are more subject to criticism, ridicule or blame, when support and understanding is more appropriate. They experience the same emotions of grief, denial, anger, bargaining, depression and acceptance. One lady who was a widow expressed to me that death of a loved one was not the worst thing, as there is finality and the person can get on with their own life.

Another module which concerned Loss and Change required us to recall early childhood memories of an emotional, physical and intellectual nature and to discuss those. This was very painful for me as I was beginning to realise that I had lost, or never had, love, affection, appreciation or approval from my mother. Memories of the conflict and arguments between my parents came flooding back. I appear to be more affected than my siblings. I considered myself lucky to be in a position to explore those difficulties through my work. It was becoming clear that all of us had repressed or frozen emotions. My sister Florence once told me that I was different every time I came home; which I now realise was true. It was inevitable that I would change due to leaving home so early, having different life experiences, working in different settings and gaining psychological knowledge. Only in my work and relationships did I feel secure. The following quotation by Artemis seems to express the loneliness and isolation that I felt: "I wish there were windows to my heart so that you could see my feelings."

There was another module about Holistic Care and Massage, which I was dubious about through lack of knowledge. I discovered to my surprise that it was very therapeutic. I derived enormous benefit from this module as I was under a lot of stress. My body was full of tension and I had not been sleeping well. As a result of the massage I began to relax and sleep better. It was time for "me", which was very therapeutic and reassuring.

Another module was on Channels of Communication. For the exercise we had to discuss earliest childhood memories of an emotional, physical and intellectual nature. This also upset me greatly as it brought back memories of my parents' turbulent relationship. It was becoming clear why I always reacted so badly when somebody corrected or criticised me; and why I was always so eager to please. I was reminded of the lack of love and not being listened to. I also recalled my first kiss when a surge of emotion passed through my body. Prior to this, I probably had not known what emotions were like and thought how we were not allowed to express our feelings, for fear of censure.

When I returned to work nothing had changed between me and Sister Smith. I was not too happy and thought of getting a transfer: but as I was planning on returning to Ireland I was biding my time and getting on with life. My emotional state was fragile and I did not take unjustified criticism well; considering that, with my input into the team, praise seemed to be more appropriate. As a result of the course I was becoming more assertive and my self-esteem was improving. I was deriving great satisfaction buzzing around London in my zany clothes, much to the amusement of the patients and I tried to ignore her attitude.

I had the support of other colleagues and my manager appreciated my work ethic and ability. We had annual assessments and when Sister Smith was doing my assessment I expressed my dissatisfaction with her input into the team. Those sentiments were felt by other members of the team also; she was not too happy to hear this. She asked me what my plans were and I told her that I was not willing to share this. I had not confided in any of my colleagues that I was planning to return to Ireland. Telling an employer that you are leaving is not the best idea as they lose interest in you and do not want to invest in any further education, and perks are also denied. I did not want anything to distract me from enjoying my career.

Moving to Ireland took a lot of organizing but I was looking forward to my new adventure, hoping that I could enjoy the sunset years of my life with my family. The housing market had not been performing well but there was good demand in my area. Prior to the encounter with Frank I was not in a position to purchase a property in Ireland without selling my house in London. It was difficult to get a mortgage in London for property in Ireland and I always felt that because I was a woman, the banks were reluctant to lend to me. It was also difficult in Ireland to get a mortgage, since my property was in London. I had no choice but to sell my property to release some capital. I was still doing well as I had bought well before the boom, plus I had had good success with renting. Initially I had planned to buy a flat for investment purposes, but it was too difficult to arrange with all my other responsibilities.

I went to Ireland to look for properties in 1996. I had to plan so that Andreas's education would not be interrupted. My family did not offer any help and I didn't sense much enthusiasm for me to return to the fold. I had to rely on friends to help. Ireland had changed and was more modern but, as I had stayed among the family when I visited I did not realise this. I was beginning to see that they were stuck in a time warp and that my mother had controlled everything. The family had got around her interference by not telling her their business, or by being economic with the truth. I started to realise why there was so much secrecy about different aspects of their lives, which should have been celebrated. As I had led an independent life and was responsible for my own decisions, I resented any interference from anybody who was not qualified to do so.

I returned to London and had to plan my move. Still worried about Frank lurking in the background, I could not put up a "For Sale" sign, which is the best way of selling. I was worried that Frank would send inappropriate clients around to harass me.

Property prices were improving; my agent was pressing me to exchange contracts, which was not necessary as this was December and I was not planning to leave until March. I did not know at the time why he was so anxious, but then discovered that his client was a business associate and he was acting more in the prospective buyer's favour than in mine. Being a woman he thought that I was gullible. I was very vulnerable as I had no one to share my responsibility.

My main concern was not to disrupt Andreas's education and I was hoping to get her back to school after the Easter break, minimising her absence from school. I was aware that it was not a good time to sell; but at that time house prices were cheap in Ireland. I had made a decision which I was happy with and wanted to follow it through. Just like all my other experiences I learned a lot from this transaction.

I went to Ireland for Christmas to check out a property which an ex-work colleague was selling. My mother's attitude was very bad and she kept arguing and watching everything I was doing. One night I stayed up reading a book just to relax; she got up and told me off for wasting electricity. I was so distressed that I thought that there must be some way to ease this pain. There was a bottle of whiskey on the table which I had brought and thought that this is just the tonic. It tasted good and had the desired effect. When I stood up to go to bed I could hardly walk. I was afraid that I would be unable to travel next day; but after some hydration I recovered and returned to London.

I sold my house and when the search was being conducted my solicitor informed me that Frank had put a charge on my property, claiming that he was owed money. He had produced plenty of bogus evidence. I asked my solicitor what was the procedure regarding removing the charge. She was economic with advice and said that she would take instructions which would cost me more money. I advised her that I would deal with this myself. I produced evidence of all the injunctions and evidence that I had to extend my mortgage and forwarded this to the Land Registry. Luckily the department replied and informed me that the charge had been cancelled. It was obvious from the evidence supplied, plus a letter of explanation that he was a fraudster. Frank was informed that he could take private action if he so desired; this did not happen as his credibility was shattered by then. Another great result. I also discovered that there had been no planning permission for an extension which had been built on my property. The planning department asked me to get on to the builder and embarrassingly I had to explain the circumstances. Luckily they were very understanding and approved the extension as it did meet with building regulations.

Work was very busy and Sister Smith announced that she was leaving after a few months. My manager informed me of this and told me that I would be deputising until a replacement was found. I was not given any choice and informed that I would not be getting an additional allowance for deputising. Financial reward did not interest me; I was always more interested in the actual work that I was doing and whether or not I found it stimulating. Leading the team did not present any difficulties as I was previously instrumental in setting up and reorganising it. To avoid being given an allowance, I would be accountable to a Sister from another team, who did not know my patients. I thought that this was an insult as it meant that I would not be attending meetings with GPs; would be unable to make instant decisions and be deprived of the status of acting in the role. I would not be involved in any of decisions or plans. I was planning to leave but this was not the time to tender my resignation, so I did not say anything but I was quietly amused. I eventually informed my manger that I was planning to take early retirement and she said that she did not think that it would be accepted, which was not correct.

The Health Service was offering early retirement to anyone who was eligible. My manager was very disappointed and said that she did not want to lose one of her best nurses. She asked me to reconsider my decision. I also had a phone call from Personnel informing me that they could not release me until a new replacement was recruited. I informed them that I was leaving the UK and had make arrangements accordingly. I was 53 years old and, in fairness, they were giving me sound advice regarding my pension contributions. If I had waited 2 more years it would be financially beneficial to me. But I had made a decision and was looking forward to starting a new chapter in my life, yet again.

As I had previously worked in other countries my pension contributions in the UK were very small. Earlier in my career it was possible to cash in pension contributions if you were leaving the country; which I did. I had no regrets about this as I had the money when I had the enthusiasm to enjoy it. At the time I just had to go as I was thinking that, as Andrea got older, she would not want to move. Also, when she went away to college, I would be left alone. Many of my friends were moving and when one gets older it is not easy to establish new friends. My colleagues were also telling me that I was making the wrong decision. Some colleagues had moved to Ireland, had not settled and had returned again, saying that the system was so different and permanent jobs were very difficult to find. Nothing would deter me as I had made my decision and would have to accept the consequences myself.

My decision left my manager with a big dilemma as there was no one suitably qualified to act in my place. Meetings were convened hastily to discuss my replacement. There was much amusement in the junior ranks as there was some division between management and junior staff. I was really sad leaving my patients as I had got to know them so well and they appreciated me so much; they had become like family to me. I just could not tell them that I was leaving. My manager asked me if I had informed them of my impending departure and I told her that I had not. In retrospect, I guess my behaviour was often unreasonable due to my circumstances and my manager had been very supportive. I do regret that I had not been more appreciative of their support. My social circumstances were not exactly compatible with my career. The staff often bore the brunt of my moods, but luckily, dealing with the patients was what often brought me to my senses. Despite all this, the staff gave me a great send off and there was a good celebration. A friend came to pick me up on the night and asked: "How can you leave this beautiful house?" I had no reservations as material things don't always make you happy and are no replacement for love.

Even though Frank had been out of my life for some time, I still had nightmares about him returning to harass me for the final time. The estate agent asked if he could put a "Sold" sign on my house and, for obvious reasons, I refused his request. I felt a great sense of relief when I got on the boat to leave for the last time in March of 1997.

Returning To My Roots

It was March of 1997 when I embarked on a journey to begin a new life in Ireland. Packing was not easy. I had accumulated so many toys, videos and children's items and I was reluctant to dispose of them for sentimental reasons. My friends suggested that I should take them with me as there was a great collection of Cyndi dolls; others suggested having a car boot sale. I had to be selective about what I brought with me. It gave me great pleasure to donate many items to playgroups in a socially deprived area and also to friends. Financial matters had to be dealt with. My car was a company car so I purchased this at a good price. Everything was going to plan and I had bought my property in Ireland. My solicitor was dealing with surveys and all was legally in order. I had mixed feelings about leaving my only permanent address: prior to this house, my permanent address was my family home in Ireland. It had sheltered my only experience of family life and the joy that came with that, brief as it may have been. It was the place where I had my most euphoric moments: when my daughter was born, watching her grow up and it changed my life in a positive way. It was the first time that I had any sense of belonging. Packing previously was simple as I had not accumulated many material possessions.

Andrea was excited about going to Ireland and her friends gave her a great send off. We had a farewell party for her friends and they were so sad to see her leave. She received farewell presents and cards and her school shirt was covered with signatures. I was really impressed by her popularity. It brought back the happy memories of all the lovely birthday parties which we had held, and also of Christmas and other celebrations. I was so anxious regarding travelling that I could not sleep.

We got up at 05:00 hours to do the final packing. The car was packed full. I had to keep enough clothes and essentials to tide us over until our luggage arrived. We also had to make space for the cat in her carrier. It was with a mixture of sadness and relief that we were finally on the road to face a six hour drive to Holyhead, then a further four hours to the west following the boat trip. I was so preoccupied with organising everything that I did not have time to think. We had to travel through the Snowdonia mountains. The traffic was usually heavy with long-distance lorries going to meet the ferry. As the road was so narrow, it was essential to give good time to get there. I had done the journey so many times before that my anxiety was alleviated a little as soon as we got on the road.

There were frequent stops as the cat meowed when she needed to get out. We arrived in Holyhead in good time to have a break and feed the cat. The journey was uneventful and we stopped off when we got to Ireland to eat, knowing that the cupboard would be bare when we got home. We arrived in the west at 8pm after a 15 hour journey. My mother did not show any great excitement, was not concerned about our long journey, nor even offered us a cup of tea. There was great anxiety and unnecessary fuss preparing for the forthcoming Station Mass in the house. My mother said: "If you are having a bath make sure not to splash as a lot of work has gone into painting and decorating." I asked did she think we had been living in a field. My siblings did not offer any assistance. I wondered if the reason for this was envy for my financial independence and achievements. Having contributed immensely to the family coffers, being supportive all my working life, the effect of this on me was disappointing to say the least.

I was anxious to move to my own home as I was feeling so uncomfortable. My mother watched every move I made. She listened in on my phone calls and relayed my business to others. I was not allowed to make phone calls, which was very unsatisfactory. She kept asking me when was I moving in to my new home? I discussed the matter with the vendor and she agreed that we could move in. There was some work which the survey had shown up and it was agreed that she would carry out this work, but unfortunately this did not happen. I was so pleased to have my independence and be able to unpack. The vendor lived locally, and was very supportive, helping me to unpack and also introducing me to local tradesmen. I suppose that I was lucky in that regard because my family did not offer much in terms of assistance.

The neighbourhood was fantastic and there were thirteen children in the village, which was wonderful for Andrea. I enrolled her in the local school; the teachers were very helpful. The school bus stopped outside our house, which was a great advantage. It was so easy as there were only five children in her class, which was a big difference from London where there were at least 20 children. The village consisted of a church, a school and a pub, with a lovely dance hall. Rural Ireland was experiencing resurgence in dancing, which was a delight for me as I had spent many happy days dancing and socialising.

I was back to the faith, fatherland and the family. Two worked out fine but the last was not quite so successful. I was so happy to be back living in the country and enjoyed looking at the animals grazing in the fields outside my door. I was reliving my childhood again. As I had trained in the local hospital, there were some people that I had previously known and they were all very welcoming and supportive. There were also people who had married into the area from where I was born. The community was very modern and active. I hosted many dinner parties and functions and invited my family. There was no "welcome home" cards or housewarming gifts except from my brother. Since there was so much emphasis on gifts for everyone when I came on holiday I found this difficult to deal with.

I resumed dancing and enjoyed the social life of the community. I had been well known for my dancing skills and people were surprised to meet me as they had not seen me for years. One said, "That looks like --- ", others said, "Oh no it can't - no it can't", then realised, "Oh begod tis." I had been out of Irish social circles for a long time but surprisingly, I got into the swing again. Little had changed and they were still playing *Hello Mary Lou*: the same tunes as I had danced to in the 60's. Our local had dances every Sunday night which were very enjoyable. My mother did not approve of me going dancing and would say, "cannabe you are going out gallivanting." She thought this activity was only for younger people. There appeared to be a moratorium on anybody being happy or enjoying themselves. It was becoming clear why my other siblings were so secretive, always fearing her disapproval.

I bought bicycles and loved the freedom of cycling around the country roads. I lived near a bog and it was beautiful on a summer's morning to walk or cycle and reminisce about my childhood days spent in the bog. I did not feel safe to ride a bike in London so this was a great novelty. The silence was fantastic: the only interruption was the singing of the birds or buzzing of the bees, the air was fresh and clean. One of the most exciting sounds was of the cuckoo, which I had not heard since my camping adventure in the Forest of Dean in Gloucestershire, some years back.

I made friends and participated in community activities. I joined the local golf club as I had always participated in some sport. This had been difficult in London for financial or logistic reasons. Joining a golf club in my earlier years would indicate a certain amount of snobbishness and affluence. There was less class distinction in the modern Ireland that I had returned to, and everybody was very welcoming and friendly.

There was always something going on in the local area: walking, festivals, waltzing competitions and an annual song contest. The River Suck Valley Walk was established and it attracts walkers from all over Ireland and abroad. Walking was becoming a big tourist industry in the west of Ireland. Not surprising as the area is very unspoiled and not commercialised. The song contest is well known internationally and many performers have become quite famous as a result of winning it. It is held annually and conducted in a very professional manner, attracting many visitors and competitors from all over Ireland. As my new address was in a different county, just over the border there is great friendly sporting rivalry. It was of great amusement to neighbours that I still put out my own county flag.

I was a single parent, which was unusual in rural Ireland in 1997. When I met neighbours from my childhood and told them of my circumstances one lady said: "Weren't you great to keep the child?" This was a surprise as I never made any secret about having a child. Others were reluctant to mention my daughter and were surprised when I spoke about her with great pride. There had been a divorce referendum a few years previously and a lot of people voted against it. One woman said it was better to be "Mrs Somebody than Mrs Nobody."

There was still a stigma for separated people but my community were very welcoming and accepted me fully. I did get some unwanted attention from the opposite sex; often from old acquaintances who were now married. The attitude had always been that if you lived in England you would be very sexually liberated. There was a joke that years ago there was no sex in Ireland before marriage but now there was no sex after marriage - at least not with your wife! Before I came home colleagues were suggesting that I should move to a city as I would never settle in the country. City life did not appeal to me and I was determined to fulfil my desire to return to my roots, which were in the country.

I was in my element discussing farming activities with the farmers and enjoying the easy going way of life. Nobody was in a hurry and there was always time to chat, which was big change from London. I found it strange that everybody spoke to you. In London, outside of the local area, you could go for hours without a greeting from anybody. When I returned to London on holiday I found it difficult to deal with the unfriendliness.

A few ladies and I cycled to Knock Shrine, which was about thirty miles away. When we got near one of the towns there was an itinerants' funeral in process. It was like a scene from the Wild West, which I found amusing. The town literally closed down for business as those events attracted large crowds, which resulted in a lot of anti-social behaviour while old scores were settled. Business people were peeping out through windows, waiting for the funeral to be over so that they could open their premises. I was back to the valley of the squinting windows! There was a large police presence but the funeral appeared to go off without incident.

Rules and regulations were very lax in the country and it was strange to see a row of cars parked on double yellow lines. I often was surprised to see people parking on the disabled bay. It did not always go down well to make any comment about those matters, as any criticism about Ireland was not welcomed. People living in rural Ireland were very parochial in their views: as they had lived there all their lives they were content with the situation. There was a St. Patrick's Day parade with floats consisting of tractors and trailers, which were different from any other city parade I had ever attended.

I got some turf cut and saved to provide fuel for the winter. Mandy, my sister asked me if I was going to have a vegetable garden. No limit to my strength or ability. Andrea's friends came from London to visit and were very good at saving the turf. She settled in well to school and the teachers and other pupils were very helpful and accommodating. It was less strict than in London. She had been going to secondary school but was not old enough to go there in Ireland. As the school year had nearly finished teachers advised that she go into fifth class, so that she would have a full school year to get used to the system. There were children from the neighbourhood in her class who were very helpful and supportive. She could have got an exemption from Irish but she didn't take it. She was aware of different languages from living a multi-cultural society and some of her friends were bilingual. I had enrolled her in Irish classes in London earlier and she had a little knowledge, plus I had liked Irish at school and would be able to help. She did well at Irish at basic level which was adequate for enrolment to university.

She had a lovely time with her neighbours; they made a play house from an old henhouse and spent many hours playing and setting it up. There were dogs, cats and farm animals, which was terrific. There was a local family who had seven children. They had a Volkswagen combi van to take them to different events. The parents took Andrea with them to discos and I was always happy that she was safe and in good company. Without the support of our good neighbours and friends our lives would have been much more difficult. When I was working I did not have to collect her late at night from discos.

Our cat was enjoying country life but unfortunately she got a prolapsed rectum and had to be put to sleep. This was very distressing for both of us. We buried her in the garden. Andrea thought that we should have got the priest to bless the grave prior to the burial. Soon afterwards I got a nice kitten which brought great pleasure. My neighbour's dogs befriended us while he was at work, so there were always pets around. Andrea also took horse riding lessons and worked at the stables some times, getting lessons in lieu of money.

My next dilemma was when Andrea went to Australia to visit her father. It was the first time I had been alone for many years. Initially I did not expect the loneliness to hit me as I thought that I would have the support of my family. A friend was in hospital in Dublin and I went to visit. I phoned my sister hoping she would invite me to stay for a few days but she said that she was too busy with her own family. My mother was aware that I was alone. Nevertheless I was not invited for Sunday lunch or other gatherings. I did have friends but friends go home at night and are not there in the morning; they also have to be entertained.

There were very few opportunities for nursing. Most of the colleagues I had trained with were now in senior positions. It was a difficult situation as I had always got positions on my own merit; it was strange for me to mix business with pleasure. A temporary vacancy became available. I was invited to go for interview and was accepted for work at the local Psychiatric unit. I was pleasantly surprised that it was so up-to-date and most of the staff were so welcoming. At the time it was rare for somebody to return after so many years abroad and some of my student colleagues were still there. I was given a temporary contract for one week, which rolled over. Being in a temporary position I had no choice in duties and my schedule was constantly changed to fit in with the demands of the unit. Andrea's grandparents were coming from Australia and I requested one week off. Staff members were saying that I was lucky to get time off so quickly which surprised me; I had not been aware of the employment conditions in Ireland. In the UK employers are pleased to fit in with the staff schedule. When the visitors left I rang to say that I was available for work but my calls were not returned.

My family did not express any interest in meeting Andrea's grandparents; which was very embarrassing as all in-laws and friends were always entertained in the family home. My mother was very jealous of the other Granny and did not always react in a pleasant manner when her name was mentioned.

I was not in a position to work at short notice or work night duty as my daughter was only twelve years old and I had to plan her care. Nursing homes were opening but the employment conditions and nursing skills required were not of interest to me. Every nursing home had to employ a qualified nurse for legal cover. One nurse who had returned from the UK went for interview to a nursing home; when she asked about the salary, the manageress said that she would be paid what they thought she was worth. There was no minimum wage at this time.

I did not seek unemployment assistance as I was expecting to find employment, but I was worried about being at home for the winter months. I learned that there was a course sponsored by the Government for unemployed people. The criterion was that you had to have signed on the dole for six months, which I had not done. I went along for the open day and explained my circumstances and I was lucky to be accepted. I was very pleased about this as I had never done anything other than nursing and did not think that I could do anything else. I thought that I would change career as the prospects of getting into a satisfactory nursing career did not appear too promising.

I commenced the course and was pleased to be a student again. I had basic knowledge of computers from my work in London and was eager to learn more. I had studied commercial subjects at school and had got good grades. I was very serious about the course but unfortunately not all shared my enthusiasm. Some unemployed people were sent there to prepare them for return to work, otherwise they would lose their benefits, but they had little interest and were often disruptive in class. In the old days in Ireland the discipline had been very strict, so this surprised me.

I enjoyed learning new subjects and I took great interest in studying. We had a good English teacher, who was also a playwright. One of our exercises was to write a short story. Not having studied English to a very high level, or having great imagination, I could only write about my own life experience. My story was about leaving Ireland. He told me that my story had a great flow, which was very encouraging. A colleague once told me that she always enjoyed getting my letters. We had a communication module and he started the lecture by asking what was the first group of people a person comes in contact with? Of course it was the family. It struck a chord with me as communication in my family always ended up in a row or disagreement. I was gaining great confidence realising that I could learn other than medically orientated subjects. I had really got most of my education through nursing. We did art and I produced some nice work, which was a surprise to myself. Other subjects were the commercial subjects which I had studied in my earlier days. I had some knowledge of computers but I was delighted to enhance my knowledge. Having had an interest in business, I enjoyed this subject. I was really pleased with the results as I got merits and distinctions in all subjects.

Christmas was coming up and I was looking forward to spending the festive season in my family home with the big open fire. I asked my mother if there were any arrangements for Christmas and she said that she was not sure. During a visit a neighbour said: "Isn't she great to be going to Dublin?" I was shocked and asked her about it and she just ignored what I said. My older sister, Mandy had arranged Christmas at her home in Dublin, without my knowledge. If I had known I would have gone to my friends in London. As a child I was always really excited about St Stephen's Day, dressing up and going out with the Wren Boys. When I was abroad I always felt sentimental on this day, as the neighbourhood was full of fun and excitement.

I was so apprehensive about Christmas but had to keep a brave face for my daughter's sake. I went to Mass on Christmas day and Andrea was excited about opening her presents. I had greeting calls from my friends overseas, which was very nice. Mandy phoned me and asked me if I was cooking a turkey. I was so overwhelmed with emotion that I started crying. I could not believe that they had excluded me from the family gathering, hearing all the activity in the background was so upsetting. Soon afterwards Florence, who lives 30 miles away, phoned inviting me to dinner. As it was 2pm it was a bit late to go anywhere. It was obvious that the two sisters had been in contact. I was particularly upset as it was the first time the light was out in the family home for years, with the exception of when my mother was in hospital. I got over that hurdle by spending time with friends and went out socialising and tried to cover up the hurt. I went to visit frequently but was never invited to the Sunday lunches with the family.

I went to London each year to conduct some business and meet up with my friends. My mother's birthday was coming up and the family, unknown to me, were arranging a big celebration in Dublin at my sister Alma's residence. I usually stayed with Mandy prior to flying. When I got there Alma phoned to invite me to the party knowing well that I would be away. It was so hurtful having to deal with such deceitful behaviour. The next Christmas I met up with a friend, Brian whom I had dated briefly in the past. I was expecting an invitation from the family for Christmas, but that did not happen. We booked to go to a restaurant with a cruise on the river Shannon. It may sound exciting but it is only exciting if that what one wants to do. I was preoccupied with what was going on at the family home and thinking of the big open fire. So needless to say it was a great relief when the day was over.

In spite of all this I kept busy and enjoyed my study and socialising. An English couple were building a house across the road, which did not please me as my lovely view of the countryside was being obstructed. It transpired that they were involved in some immoral activities not in keeping with rural Ireland. *The Sunday World* newspaper got wind of events and carried the story with a big headline:

Hooker said: "I'll dress in black, the real Princess Di look alike."
We track down sick vice girl and pimp husband who shame the memory of Diana.
Sleepy Village in the West Rocked by Revelations.

There was a photograph of the partially built property. There was a constant presence of reporters looking for information. RTÉ gave the story prominence on its airwaves, stating that revelations of the couple's antics are sure to shock the tiny rural community in the west of Ireland.

Not being fully aware of prying eyes and lenses I was sunbathing in the front garden in my swimsuit. I now realise that the dress code was not exactly appropriate for rural Ireland. A local lady who had previously returned from the UK advised me that it was not the best thing to do, as there were reporters about. There was some surveillance on my house as the couple in question had lived there prior to me. As I was also a returned immigrant I might have got tarred with the same brush; in fact some narrow minded people did suggest that I might engage in similar activities.

There were photographs on the paper which caused great anger, as it brought unwanted attention to the quiet rural area. The partially built property was constantly watched by the press for activity. The couple were living in a rented house locally and every move they made was monitored by the press. The phone numbers given advertising their services were constantly checked. As a result of the publicity and constant harassment, the couple left the area unannounced. Nobody knew what was happening to their property. The neighbours, who were unhappy with all the publicity, began to distance themselves from the couple. It was uncomfortable for their two sons who did not know what was going on.

I got the idea of purchasing their unfinished house. The housing market was improving and the Celtic Tiger was making his presence felt. I had some money left over from the sale of my house in London and was getting hungry for a challenge. I made enquiries from the estate agent and he told me that the property was for sale. I put in an offer which was accepted; to my surprise, there was no competition. There were some complications as the property was being built by direct labour and the builder had now left. Luckily, with legal advice the problem was solved.

Since I was an unemployed single parent there was curiosity as to why I should buy another house and also how could I afford it. I did not know how things operated in the country; otherwise I may not have got involved. In retrospect the play by J. B. Keane, *The Field*, comes to mind. There were people interested but were afraid to get involved due to the history. Also if anybody was interested, nobody else would interfere because of tradition and loyalty; but I was new to the area and did not realize all of this. As I did not have a permanent job I was unable to get a mortgage. I did not have the finances to develop the property but had seen the potential. I knew that if I could not develop it myself, I could sell it on as is. I was becoming very interested in property development and exercising my entrepreneurial skills.

The feeling of resentment, exclusion, criticism and demands from my family created stress and tension with the result that I developed irritable bowel syndrome. I went to my GP and was referred immediately for further investigation. The consultant said that it was stress related. At the time I did not agree as I had so much stress and challenges in my life previously. I had an endoscopy and further tests which confirmed that there was no abnormality. I could deal with most situations and found it frustrating that I was unable to deal with the demands of my family. I was not aware that their attitude was affecting me so deeply. I thought my problem was food related. I recalled having similar symptoms when I came on family visits and did not connect it with the conflict. Any attempt to discuss my emotional issues with my siblings were quickly dismissed.

I was treated for this and decided to seek psychological help privately. I was recommended to a doctor out of area, following a consultation we concluded that my circumstances were very stressful. She prescribed anti-depressants, which was not exactly what I was expecting. She was very reassuring and said that I should be so proud of my many wonderful achievements. She pointed out that it was obvious that I was different from my other siblings and that there was some envy and jealousy. This was useful and helpful information.

I complied with the treatment for a few weeks. I was aware from my own medical knowledge that chemical intervention just gives temporary relief and issues will resurface later. It was becoming clear that my problems were very deep-seated and required a different approach. At the time I felt so put down by my family that I could not appreciate my own achievements. Relations and neighbours were very complimentary; they admired my independence and achievements not that they knew all of it. I was playing a multifunctional role: breadwinner, mother, father, in addition to setting up and maintaining a new home. The lack of approval and inclusion was becoming very distressing. Everybody likes praise and acceptance, particularly when it is well earned and deserved.

I wrote to the doctor and told her that I felt better and would not continue to see her again. I had to be careful not to have such consultations on my record as it would jeopardise my chances of getting work in medicine. Living in rural Ireland I could not discuss this with anybody and did not want to display any weakness. Away from my family I appeared to be very happy and doing well; but secretly this was not so. Rejection and disapproval were taking its toll.

In Ireland

I had heard that there was a post for a community nurse for weekend relief. I had been living mostly from my savings and was anxious to get back to nursing as I missed it so much. Prior to this there were very few opportunities; nurses tended to stay in the same position for years. As a result most of the new graduates had no choice but to emigrate. Like many other Irish nurses they did not return: employment prospects, opportunities for promotion and training were much better abroad. I had experience working in many areas: Psychiatry, Community Care and General Nursing. My first reply was from a geriatric home which was run by the health board. I went for interview in June 1999 and was called to work immediately.

My first day was relieving the nurse in charge of the day care area, which I really enjoyed. Then I was called to work in the in-patient area. It was not my area of choice but in rural Ireland nursing positions were hard to find and beggars cannot be choosers. I had not worked in a hospital for years; my work in London was in the community and quite specialised. Most of the staff had been there for years and I was the first new face in a long time.

Being new to the scene, people were eager to know my history and asked personal questions. I had not worked with an all-Irish staff for many years and found that "slagging" was still part of the culture. I often got upset at some of the comments that were made which were meant to be fun. My attitude, accent, and terminology were different; my social circumstances were also unusual. My credentials were not in keeping with rural Irish thinking, but it appeared I was accepted. I had known some of the staff from school days.

I could not believe that nurses were working below their level of endeavour as there were no nursing assistants. The Doctor had to be consulted for clinical decisions: which was so different from in the UK. There was no continuing education or clinical updates unless a nurse paid for same. In the UK you could not register unless you did a certain amount of study days. I was reduced to doing menial nursing tasks which did not give much job satisfaction. My role was that which I had done as a student nurse several years before. It was surprising that so little had changed in thirty years absence. The other nurses appeared happy with the situation, as employing nursing assistants could create less nursing positions. I had always looked on nursing as a career, but it now appeared that it was a job.

I was employed to work one week on and one week off to cover maternity leave, which suited my circumstances. I was not given any employment information and later discovered that I should be signing on the unemployment register for the week when my services were not required. I requested not to do night duty as my daughter was only twelve and could not be left alone at night.

Nurses were demanding more pay and a strike/work to rule ensued. Salaries in the UK were much less and I could not understand this. The Celtic Tiger was raising its ugly head. I had never known a strike/work to rule to take place in my career and was not in favour of this. Even though it was my week off I had to work to rule despite my agreement not to do nights. I was assigned to work night duty without pay which upset me greatly as I was only a temporary nurse. I objected and this did not meet with the approval of the permanent staff. I was told that I should do what was requested of me. I declined and did not do it. Eventually the strike/work to rule was settled and all went back to work as usual. Nurses were given 2 days extra leave, but when

I enquired about this I was informed that I did not qualify as I was only temporary. Considering I did not want to participate in the strike/work to rule I was pretty disappointed. There was a financial settlement and improvement in terms and conditions.

There was a lot of resentment towards nurses returning from abroad and new faces were under great scrutiny. I thought that my experience and knowledge would have been an asset and I could see that improvements could be made. I was very naïve in thinking like this as there was a "do not rock the boat" syndrome and any comments or suggestions were unwelcome. I found out that if you wanted to work you had to keep your mouth shut, which was difficult to bear.

At this time the Health Service was greatly underfunded in this particularly area. This facility had been run by nuns for many years and stories told that were not all too complimentary. The building had been a night shelter for the homeless and down and outs. It dated back to famine times. It was also a facility for girls who had children out of wedlock and the stories were very disturbing. All this was accepted at the time, or not talked about

The terms and conditions for nurses in Ireland were a big surprise to me. I was beginning to understand why other colleagues who came home, returned to the UK after they found they could not tolerate the system. Nurses worked for several years on temporary contracts, some of them for fifteen years or more. They got no holidays or sick leave and their contracts were frequently broken, depriving them of those rights. If a face did not fit, or asked too many questions, they were put on a waiting list and not called back to work, as a lesson to be quiet. As I was a new nurse and was temporary I could not request any holidays and had to be on call whenever I was needed. There was a staff meeting and I asked some questions; I heard afterwards about the "new nurse asking questions" and the "ink not dry on her contract." It was so demoralising that the wisdom and knowledge

I gained abroad was not acknowledged. I was a "new", temporary nurse and what would I know. There was double pay for Sundays and bank holidays, all the permanent nurses worked those shifts and temporary nurses did not. Less attractive shifts were given to the temporary nurses. Nurses were given an extra day off following a stint of night duty; this applied only to permanent staff even though the temporary staff did the same duties. In my previous experience nurses preferred not to work weekends and bank holidays, but because of the added incentives there was great demand for working anti-social hours. It was difficult to accept those conditions and I expressed my opinions which were not welcome.

In 1999 I went to work on Christmas Eve morning; one of the night duty permanent nurses went on sick leave. I was pressurised into going home at 11 am and return for night duty that night. As a temporary nurse I realised that I did not have much choice. I was not happy to do this because of my circumstances but if I refused I would not have any work. I was hoping that I would be working on her rota and agreed reluctantly to do as requested. I had to make child-minding arrangements. I worked that night and came off duty on Christmas day and was not given further employment.

I had no work all over Christmas and New Year and there was a great shortage of staff. This treatment for nurses who spoke out was not unusual. Change was resented, which presented difficulty for me due to my experience. The permanent care assistants appeared to have more acknowledgement than temporary nurses. It was the first time in my long and varied career that I had experienced dissent and disrespect in the workplace. Comments such as, "If London was so great why did she return home?" were made. Working in a small country town it would be difficult to get a reference if you fell foul of the matron.

As the economy started to improve more money was becoming available and vacancies were filled on a permanent basis. I had no particular interest in working in this field of medicine but decided to go for interview for the sake of experience. My preference was to get into the acute nursing field but there were no opportunities at the time. I submitted my application and was the most qualified and experienced nurse. I performed well at interview and was surprised that out of sixteen nurses I was not successful in my application for a permanent position. I was so demoralised to be turned down for a position for which I was overqualified, that I did not have the confidence to seek employment elsewhere. I did not know why I was rejected, apart from expressing my opinion, which was unfair. There was no question about my nursing ability, as I used my initiative and skills to do some very worthwhile challenging nursing duties.

The word spread rapidly and I was the topic of conservation and gossip. I tendered my resignation to matron who accepted it without comment. I discovered later that as I had a temporary contract which stated "if and when", that I did not have to work one month's notice but matron did not tell me this. I suppose she was shocked, as it was unusual for somebody to leave, due to the shortage of nursing positions. Apparently it was the custom when a stint of work was completed, to make an appointment with matron and say, "thank you very much for the work and I will be available for work whenever you need me." I was horrified on hearing this and needless to say did not do it; therefore I was not number one on the popularity list for grovelling.

As it happened there was a great shortage of nurses which put enormous pressure on the existing staff. Matron said that she could not find anybody. She was reminded that I available. Word was sent to me via colleagues to contact her. I did this and was offered whatever hours suited me. I was re-employed on another temporary contract. Luckily there was a new manager on the ward who had progressive ideas, which pleased me and my contribution was appreciated. The work load was very heavy and staff were under a lot of stress. Soon afterwards I hurt my back due to the heavy workload and had to take holidays so that I did not break my service: I had not earned enough stamps to get sick pay. I also learned afterwards that there were procedures in place for "injury at work" which I was not been made aware of.

Soon after this there was a change of management and, with union representation I was appointed to a permanent position. I requested details of my initial interview and was shocked to see that I was given minimum marks and previous experience not acknowledged. I was then eligible for all the benefits and pension rights. With permanent work guaranteed I was in a position to start completing my building project. Mortgaging a partially built property was not possible so I had to build it as I earned. I was introduced to very good builders and work commenced. It was a great challenge and source of enjoyment to coordinate the project. It was finally finished and I moved in in 2000 with help from my partner. As I lived across the road I moved in gradually and it was not too stressful. Just like all the other events in my life, I didn't think anything of it and just got on with it.

It was then necessary to prepare my existing home for sale. I had to get a new septic tank as the existing one never functioned properly. The property boom was starting and due to the influx of immigration there was a greater demand for housing. The more houses that were built the more labour was required and the more houses were required to accommodate them. It was very difficult to sell my house as a lot of work needed to be done to update it to modern standards. Eventually, after several viewings, it was sold, not at a great profit, but taking into consideration that I had lived there for a few years, I felt that I had broken even. I did learn valuable lessons from the whole transaction.

Andrea was anxious to get a puppy. Secretly I had always harboured the desire to have a dog like I had when I was young. I recalled pleading with my mother to keep the stray puppy and was overjoyed when she finally agreed. I observed that my neighbour's dog was pregnant. It was a surprise as the dog was six years old and very tiny, hence the name. The pregnancy was uneventful and she loved plenty of attention. When my neighbour was at work she would come over to our place. She was so tiny that when the pregnancy advanced she could hardly walk. It was difficult to determine the due date. I went on holiday and was hoping that I would be back for the event. She had delivered 5 puppies in my absence, unfortunately four died and we took the one that survived. When Andrea came from school I had the puppy waiting for her, she was so pleased and excited. She got the choice of naming him and decided to call him Bailey. He gave us great pleasure and it was fun teaching him tricks and taking him for walks. One day he got killed by a freak accident. It was devastating and we were all so upset as he was just reared. We got another puppy soon afterwards which was so exciting as well as consoling.

Shortly after I was admitted to hospital for minor surgery; I was scared and very worried. My concern was for the welfare of Andrea if anything should happen to me. I needed a lot of reassurance and support as I had never been ill or an in-patient in hospital previously. I informed Mandy but she did not offer the support I was hoping for; instead she advised me not to tell Mammy as she would be upset. The matter was never discussed further within the family and I did not want to suffer any further rejection by telling any of them. I relied on my partner, friends and work colleagues for support. I was looked after superbly by the staff and made a full recovery. I remember a nurse whispering in my ear prior to anaesthetic: "Don't worry; we will look after you well." Her kindness was quite overwhelming. The nurses were amused that I was out of bed so quickly and was so independent. I was greatly relieved that my prayers had been answered and the outcome was satisfactory.

The economy was improving at a great rate in 2003 and the property market was starting to boom. I was getting hungry for another challenge and decided to purchase another property. I was in a position to get a mortgage because I had secure employment and was lucky to find a nice property in the local town. It was in good condition but needed painting and furnishing to prepare it for renting. There was a great demand for rented accommodation due to the number of immigrants who were entering the country. The property boom was like what had happened in London with everybody wanting to get on the property ladder. As demand increased so did the prices. I furnished the property and had no difficulty in getting tenants.

My life was reasonably satisfying and I was enjoying going on holiday with my partner. One holiday was to Tunisia; when I saw the desert and heard the language I felt very sentimental. Another trip was to Penang in Malaysia. I stood on the bridge that had been wiped out by the tsunami soon after. I regularly went on a culture trip to London and to see my friends. I enjoyed going there as it was so familiar and nostalgic. I went to see so many shows in the West End: *Billy Elliot, Mama Mia, Hairspray, We will Rock You* were all showing, which were very enjoyable. Andrea was in her last year at school and I was apprehensive about her leaving home and being alone again. My colleagues at work were so supportive and reassuring, which was a great help. She was accepted at the University in Galway to study science subjects. She had been my companion for 18 years and it was hard to believe she was leaving home. Of course she was excited about being with new friends and moving to the city. I was in a state of bewilderment as I did not know how I would cope with living alone. The house was so lonely now that I had no one to look after. I did as much night duty as was possible and was out most of the time. It took several weeks to get used to being alone but, like always, I just had to get on with life. I had dogs and a cat which provided a little security and company.

I was finding my work physically demanding and decided to apply for a transfer to the Acute Sector. It was amazing the difficulty I had in doing this. I had been in contact with personnel and they assured me that when a vacancy arose I would have first preference. I was given a date to transfer. My manager said that she could not release me until there was a replacement. Nurses from overseas were recruited and were due to arrive. I was not happy about this and did express my opinion; eventually I was released.

My property was rented to an elderly couple who were returned emigrants. The estate agent was collecting the rent and, I understood, was managing it. All went well for a while. I checked in on them frequently as they were in poor health. They were good tenants initially but then they had dogs which they kept in the house. The dogs were big and as a result, I did not go into the house but communicated with them on the doorstep. It appeared that all was going well. Eventually they expressed an interest in purchasing the property, to which I was agreeable. It was the height of the property boom and I thought it would be exciting to move on to another project. The tenant said that he wanted to buy the property for his son who had received compensation following an accident. I met the son and it all sounded very plausible. Soon, however, there were complaints from the neighbours about his behaviour. He had several old cars in the garden. The dogs were often allowed to wander outside, which was disturbing their peace. I went to speak to them and was given reassurance that they would try to resolve their issues. The tenants kept telling me that the son was made a ward of court and the money could not be released until his condition improved.

There was an enormous building boom and houses were springing up all over the country, with housing estates in every village and town. Many people had returned from abroad and this further fuelled the building boom. I was in London during the housing boom and the topic of every conversation was about house prices. History was repeating itself and the main topic of conversation was house prices; only with an Irish twist of negativity, envy and begrudgery.

It was 2006 I was getting impatient with my tenant as the date for release of the money was constantly being deferred. I decided to purchase a flat in the local town. As my finances were tied up in property I approached the credit union for a bridging loan. I made enquiries and was told that I would have to meet with the directors. The interview was arranged and the meeting went well, with the manager saying that my credit rating was good and the staff gave me a good reference. In view of my age however, he said that would have to confer with his colleagues. I waited for a few days and he contacted me to say that the loan had been approved. The agreement was that there would be a charge on my property, which meant the loan would be paid off when the sale was complete. I negotiated a deal for the purchase of the flat, even though there was a downturn in property prices. People were getting cautious about investing because of the uncertainty in the market but some people had to sell for different reasons. The economists predicted a soft landing and I was hoping that there would be a recovery. There were tenants in the flat, which suited me perfectly and all I had to do was issue a new contract.

Some problems arose with my rented property. I had a call from the police to say there were problems and they wished to gain entry. They did not enlighten me and I did not know what was going on. I had visions of TV cameras arriving and getting exposed once again to publicity. My initial thought was that my family would hear; not all of them knew about my purchase. The tenant had abandoned the house, leaving his dogs to run wild. It appears that he had not lived there for some time, but kept his dogs there and visited frequently to feed them. I had been talking to him frequently on his mobile regarding the purchase, but he had not said that he had left. Not the first time the mobile let me down. I understood that the Estate Agent was managing the property, but when the problem arose he informed me that he was providing a rent collection service only. From discussions with them during the tenancy I did not get that impression. The contract was very vague. The tenant was receiving housing benefit, which he paid to the agent from where it was paid directly into my bank account.

The stress and disappointment was enormous. The police were more concerned about his personal effects than about my house. I also felt that I was the one who was under suspicion. I later discovered that the tenant had been in trouble with the law and he and his wife abandoned the property and fled to the UK. My solicitor was away and I was in a very distressed state. There was nothing I could do. I felt so angry and disappointed as I had been so helpful to them.

I decided, with advice from my solicitor, that if they had not been in contact after one month I would start clearing the property. I tried several times to contact the tenant but there was no reply from his phone. The police advised against disposing of their property but with advice from my solicitor I was prepared to take the risk. In retrospect it was the right decision. The sale did not take place and I did not have any contact with the tenant or his son since they left the property.

My friend Ann was coming from London, which provided some welcome distraction. We went on a trip to Northern Ireland, which I really enjoyed. We travelled along the Antrim coast where the scenery was magnificent. We saw the Giants Causeway, which was very interesting and walked on the

Carrick-a-Rede Rope Bridge. It was marvellous to get away from my natural habitat and a welcome distraction from the problem. I was not really looking forward to coming home to face the ordeal, but it had to be done.

It took several weeks to clear and clean the property. I just did not want to discuss the problem with anybody, as what people say is often too insensitive. Hindsight is a great thing and of course things could have been done differently. My partner was very supportive and recommended people to help with the laborious part. Several boxes of empty alcohol bottles had to be removed; it was embarrassing taking the bottles to the recycling centre as I rarely drink alcohol. The recession had hit and there was no problem getting labour. I just kept thinking that no matter what happened it could be worse, nobody died. People were saying what a lovely house it was and my reply was "it will be lovely again."

I just decided to be positive and turn disaster into a challenge. It was a good opportunity to modernise the property and prepare it for sale. It was a great learning curve as I had pleasure in organising builders, tradesmen and gardeners to do the work. It was a very interesting project and occupied a lot of my spare time. I was also proud that my business skills had been tested and were successful. I turned a predicament into an achievement. I met many good people during the project which was some compensation. The property market was stagnant and I was unable to sell, but fortunately there was great demand for renting. I have had very good tenants in the meantime.

My brother John, who lived in London, was interested in purchasing a property, planning for his retirement. I was pleased to give him information and guidance. He bought a property in the local town which he was happy with. The housing boom was escalating and it was very difficult to get tradesmen to do work.

Promises would be made but would not come to fruition. They would say, they will come tomorrow but it did not always happen. I arranged to have to furniture fitted and make it in a habitable condition where he could relax for his holidays. Patience is a very useful commodity when you live in the country. Unfortunately I did not have that but have learned from experience.

I continued to visit my mother and provided as much support and advice as possible, which she did not appear to appreciate. Her attitude was very upsetting and I was excluded from many family events. I was often very embarrassed when colleagues at work asked if I was going to spend Christmas with my mother. Grandchildren and family came to visit but I was never made aware of impending visits. Sometimes I accidently gate-crashed some of those visits, which caused me embarrassment and distress.

She was not coping well and eventually agreed to go to a nursing home in 2006. My advice was sought due to my knowledge of the service. When I went to visit her she was very unpleasant, which really upset me. I was aware, from my own knowledge, that staff would monitor the interaction of family, which made me uncomfortable. I decided with professional advice not to visit . She was in the nursing home for more than one year. My siblings did not visit me, knowing that it would not meet with her approval. My nieces and nephews were visiting her but I was not invited or aware of their visits. The only contact was by phone to seek advice about different issues which arose in the family. Mandy phoned me and insisted that I go to visit her as her condition was deteriorating. I was planning to go when, at 07:00 hours, my brother-in-law phoned to say that she had died at five that morning. I was silent. I felt no emotion and asked what he wanted me to do, that I did not want to go to the nursing home alone. He agreed to meet me there at 9 am. I phoned work and informed them of the situation and got there promptly. I was very apprehensive, not knowing how I was going to feel; or what would be the reaction of the other siblings. I was embarrassed going into the nursing home as I had not visited for some time. When I got there she just looked as though she was asleep, her colour was good. My thoughts were racing and I felt that this is the first time that she did not shout at, ignore or upset me. Being a very spiritual, good-living person, it occurred to me "that the powers that be" intervened and saved me from a terrible roasting. I shed a few tears of relief. The removal was planned for 2 pm. I sat with her until then and found it so peaceful and comforting. It was ironic that she had died without any member of the family present, despite having controlled her children all of her life. The family gradually arrived; there was no great show of grief or emotion. We all went to the local restaurant. I kept a low profile and did not say too much, fearing some outburst of hostility. Normally she was the one to give all the instructions and her decisions were final; consequently there was an absence of leadership. Some arrangements were made, which had to be changed as some of the family lived overseas and could not be there in time. My advice was sought about the funeral arrangements and other issues which I would have been familiar with. I was pleased that my contribution was requested and glad to be included. Communication was not something that was done in a civilised manner in my family.

I asked Mandy if the family home would be open for neighbours to visit. She said that would be impossible at it was not used, was cold and that it was too small to accommodate the amount of people who would be attending. I was not happy about this and suggested that we go and check it out. We got there, put on a fire, cleaned it up and it was ready in no time. All the neighbours and family assembled there. I later heard from relatives that it was a great compliment to the family for doing such a lovely thing. I thought that it was a fitting way to end the many years of activity in the busy family home. Everybody was very sentimental about the fact that a long and great chapter had closed. There was a great night of reminiscence therapy.

I was looking forward to being part of the family and thought that I had earned their approval and respect. I was hoping that I would be included in all family activities, which I always longed for. When the coffin was being closed for the final time, I was expecting a great show of grief from my sisters, but that was not the case. I did not feel any emotion but did show respect. My hopes of family unity were short lived when my brother-in-law introduced me to his son's fiancée as the "wicked witch from the west." They found this amusing but I was deeply hurt and said so. No apology given and I was told that I should accept it in the way in which it was intended.

Mandy suggested that we all get our own flowers. I gave the matter some thought and decided that, as I had never pleased my mother in life, it would be unlikely to happen now. I was concerned that friends, relations and neighbours would notice if I didn't provide a bouquet. Having a good sense of humour I hatched up a plan. I stood close enough to the hearse to be given a big bouquet of flowers to carry walking up to the church. I repeated the performance on the day of internment. I was bursting to share the joke with my friends but knew that it would be inappropriate.

I was pleasantly surprised to see so many of my friends, colleagues and neighbours present. My family also commented on the great number that came to offer their condolences on my behalf. I just thought, 'If she could only see my popularity, she would be surprised.' There was a beautiful Mass and the priest delivered a very complimentary homily about her; as they do for all deceased. One of my colleagues, who was a little aware of my relationship with her, said that he spoke well of her. I replied: "If he only knew the whole story." The burial took place and I was really surprised that very little tears were shed. This was probably due to the fact that we were never allowed to show emotion. I walked away from the graveyard with a great sense of calm, relief and emotional freedom. It was an end to 64 years of emotional turmoil. Task completed, we all adjourned to the local hotel for the "last supper", compliments of her funeral fund. I was pleased that all had gone off so well. It was an opportunity to meet my nieces, nephews and a new baby whom I had not seen for some time.

We spent the remainder of the day at the family home which provided a great sense of comfort and finality. I talked to Mandy and said that she was now head of the family and it was up to her to keep us together. I gave her a letter and a spiritual card about listening and was hopeful that she would feel some obligation to do so.

Andrea went back to work and, after all the activity I felt a great sense of loneliness. I was on compassionate leave, plus time off, for eleven days, but I wanted to be with people. I had previously made arrangements for a reunion with some of my travelling friends, to be held in Dublin on the Wednesday following the internment. I just wanted to get away from the house and be with people, so I decided that a break to reflect and support from my friends would be very therapeutic, which it was. I felt embarrassed that I did not show any sadness for the loss of my mother. It must have been difficult for them to understand why I should not show some emotion. When I had known them many years before, issues about my family were never discussed and I always appeared so carefree and happy. I did not want to spoil the reunion and there was no further discussion about her demise.

I returned to work and was happy to be back to where I had always felt secure and appreciated. The next family meeting was for the Month's Mind - a requiem mass celebrated one month after a person's death in memory of the deceased. There was a party for family and friends at the local community centre which was nice. I was expecting that the family would get together for Christmas and move on and forget the past. Unfortunately this did not happen to my great disappointment. They did not express any gratitude for my contributions to the arrangements and support given.

I learned from a book, *Death Benefits*, written by American psychotherapist, Jeanne Safer that death of a parent can be strangely liberating. She says that losing a parent may be the best thing that ever happened to you. The book is part autobiographical and part based on interviews with 60 mid-life men and women, who discovered unexpected "death benefits" following the passing of their elderly parents. It also recounts the often tortured relationship that she endured with her mother, whose manipulative behaviour was the cause of deep anxiety which, despite her professional training as a psychotherapist, she struggled to control as an adult. Her mother died when she was 92 years old; my mother died when she was 94 years old. She too had lived away from her mother since she was 17 years old. Many of the adult children she interviewed had difficult parents, who were emotionally distant or abusive and keen to find fault with their children, no matter how successful they were. This all made great sense to me.

Some issues arose in the family which is not my story to tell. I was inundated with phone calls from my sisters for advice and support. Because of my cosmopolitan life experience, they depended on me for support and advice on most issues. I was helpful and gave as much support as I could. As usual, when the issues were temporarily resolved the phone calls stopped. I was always there for the pain but never for the pleasure. I felt very angry and was aware that I needed psychological support.

I was having lunch with a professional colleague and we were discussing different issues. The issue of my mother's death arose and after some discussion I realised that it was appropriate to seek professional help. I had been contemplating seeking emotional support/ bereavement counselling for some time but was too proud to admit that I could not deal with my problems. The issue of the relationship with my mother was discussed in more detail. The family dynamics were also discussed and she asked, jokingly: "Where did they get you?" She said that because of my being so different and independent that I would never fit in. Her suggestion was to concentrate on the positive aspects of my life and move on.

I had a good friend in London who also had mother issues. She became a mature student and qualified as a psychologist. She was a great source of strength and support. She pointed out that my family had bullied me and disrespected me, and that also needed to be explored. I realised that this was true. I was constantly looking for answers and found great strength in my spirituality. I always liked going to Sunday Mass and my curate gave lovely homilies about different issues. One time he said: "You can change the sail but you cannot change the gale." I had to move on and make the best of the present and the future.

Retirement

The next life changing experience was my retirement in February 2009. I was so grateful that I had completed my career of forty-seven years with an unblemished record, despite all my traumas. I had worked in eight different countries and travelled to thirty-nine. I had the pleasure of working in so many different cultures and various nursing settings. Nursing had provided me with the opportunity to travel the world.

Initially I did not want to discuss the implications of retirement. I had been so work dependent and just could not imagine how I would cope without the support of my colleagues and the milieu of my work place. The only true focal point I had in my life, until I had my daughter, was my career: my career was my family. I was worried that I would not cope with the isolation or lack of the routine of working life. At the time I was the oldest staff member at the Psychiatric unit and new staff were being employed. I knew it was time to go as the role of a nurse was becoming more academic. I was more interested in the clinical side of nursing and face to face contact.

Initially when I retired it was great not having any commitment or having to get up in the morning. The novelty of this soon wore off and I felt lost. I would often return to visit my old workplace and still felt part of the team. I guess I was in denial that I had actually retired. I joined a yoga class, which was very therapeutic and met some new people. It was easier to plan a social life and do things of choice which were impossible when doing shift work. I had to establish a routine and went swimming and to the gym. I enjoyed visiting neighbours and relations from my childhood, who were now elderly. Sadly they were dying but I was pleased that I was there for their funerals. I was not too despondent and was always hopeful. I had dual qualifications and would not have difficulty getting employment as an agency nurse if I so desired; but to my great surprise, as soon as I left I had no desire at all to do nursing. In retrospect I have difficulty believing how I fitted in so many other activities and have a full-time career. Looking back I was in a state of anxiety most of the time and depended on my career for support and appreciation.

There was a demand for volunteering. I made enquiries and went to a meeting; they expressed great interest in my services. I insisted that I would not be interested in doing any nursing duties. The vetting procedures were strict and I found it as difficult as getting employment, only the responses were faster. I had previously discovered when I returned to Ireland, that applications for employment were often ignored. As I had worked in so many countries it was requested that I provide details of all my residential addresses since my birth. I explained that this procedure had been carried out when I returned to Ireland and I had only worked for the Health Board since then. My residential address had been the same. They were not happy with this explanation. I had lived in hotels, youth hostels, nurse's homes and had forgotten most addresses anyway. I abandoned this idea but several months later received a letter to say that I had been accepted. I declined as by this stage I was enjoying getting involved in social activities and making new friends.

I was coping with retirement much better than expected. I occupied my time by travelling and visiting friends. I had done so much travelling that I had no desire to go further than London. I was surprised at the attitude from others regarding my retirement: questions like, "what are you going to do to pay back?" or "you have so much more to give."!

In a further search for peace of mind I went on a pilgrimage to Lough Derg. Unfortunately I hurt my toe but was told by another penitent that I would get an extra indulgence because of this. I did complete the full pilgrimage but with some discomfort - never one to give up! I had done this pilgrimage many years before and did not expect it to be so difficult. Of course I was much younger then. I also attended a pre-Christmas retreat. The homily was about forgiveness. I approached the priest in a rather confrontational manner and asked him how I could forgive somebody who had caused me so much emotional pain, and affected my life in such a negative way. He was a bit taken back at my attitude and asked me to pray with him for forgiveness. It did help somewhat but not fully.

I had often thought, during my years of working in England, of travelling from London to Ireland by bus. But at that time it was not practical due to the time constraints and also I needed my car when I got home. I decided that it would be a good idea do the reverse journey from Ireland to London and was excited about the adventure. With all the security issues and restrictions at the airport, I thought going by bus would be less stressful. The initial part of the journey was good but the bus driver stopped off every few hours on the motorway and it was impossible to sleep. I arrived in London in a very exhausted state. I had a sleep for a few hours and got on with my holiday. The return journey was fine until we got to Dublin. The bus connection to my area was not very satisfactory which prolonged the time. I had been travelling for twenty hours and I thought it would never end. I will not be travelling by bus to London again but my curiosity has been satisfied.

I decided to do a psychology course but discovered it was raising too many emotional issues, so I discontinued with it. Christmas was also approaching, which always causes me some anxiety. I kept busy with social activities and joined a book club.

I never had time to concentrate on reading; which is now a great source of contentment for me. I also joined a creative writing class, which is very enjoyable and stimulating. During summer I enjoy gardening and the upkeep of my property. I enjoy playing golf and other sports. In my town there is a theatre festival which is held annually and there are great productions during the winter months, which I enjoy immensely.

One of the great pleasures in my life was my dog called Frodo, who sadly died. It was devastating as she was only six years old. I depended on her for security as, when she heard a sound outside, she barked furiously. When she got ill I took her to the vet. She did some tests and discovered that she had severe diabetes and Cushing's syndrome. The vet said that she could stabilise her but that she would be on insulin, a strict diet and other medications for life. This would be a problem as she went to my neighbour and got treats and also ate the cat's food. She also went there when I went on holiday as it was convenient. It was totally unexpected as she appeared healthy. The vet recommended that it was best, with my consent, to put her to sleep. I agreed to this and it was nice that I was with her in her last minutes. I preferred that ending than for her to be knocked down by a car or to go missing.

I was on my own and was worried about burying her, but fortunately my neighbour was just coming from work and assisted in the burial. It all happened so quickly that I did not have time to think about it. Later that night I was afraid to go to sleep; the house was so quiet and my security blanket had gone. Another great loss in my life and nobody to share the burden! I had planned to get another dog but was waiting for my daughter to come home to select one. I gave it some thought and decided not to replace her, as it was too much of a commitment when I went away.

Having had time to reflect on my life, I am proud that I had such varied and often exciting experiences. I am grateful to all the nice people who have been so supportive to me along the way. I also have to apologise to the partners that I may have unintentionally hurt. The only regret I do have is that I did not get married and have more children, as I had planned in my earlier years. My peers and siblings are enjoying their grandchildren, which is what I would have liked as I love children and sharing the excitement of a big happy family. I recall the overwhelming desire I had to have a child and I often get the same feeling when my friends talk about their grandchildren. I am grateful that I was brave enough to ignore my mother and have one child, who has given me so much enjoyment and satisfaction. One day I hope I will be lucky enough to have the pleasure of grandchildren.

Andrea is happy, well-adjusted independent girl. She has many friends and really enjoys life. She did not complete her University course but returned later and qualified as a Veterinary Nurse. She is in constant contact with her father, goes to Australia to visit and spends long periods working there. She also meets him when he visits Europe. I have no idea what happened to Frank but it fills me with horror when I think of that period of my life. In retrospect I feel a great sense of achievement that I outwitted him.

Even though I had a terrific career and life abroad I never really felt 'at home'. I guess I stayed away for obvious reasons, but I am so pleased that I was in a position to return with my daughter to my own roots, where I feel more comfortable and secure within my own culture and traditions. There is no wit like the Irish wit and the pace of living suits me perfectly. In London, when you meet somebody new, you get asked where you live and what school your child goes to: this appears to determine your status. In rural Ireland every child goes to the same school and everybody is the same; your status is determined by your own character, behaviour and personality.

Even though I faced many emotional challenges, I feel very privileged to have been part of the Irish Diaspora. I had so many experiences which would not be possible living in the very restricted society of my earlier years, with fear of being ostracised. My culture and identity are important to me. In the US, when Americans heard that you were Irish, they claimed to be Irish despite never having been to Ireland. They were the offspring of families who emigrated during famine times and since then, but still claimed to be Irish. At the time I found this fascinating.

Living in the UK there are so many Irish people. Also, Ireland is so near the UK it was like living in another province of Ireland. It is a little confusing for relations of Irish people who were born in the UK: they speak with English accents, have Irish names, are proud of their Irish heritage and consider themselves Irish. They still move in Irish circles and obey Irish traditions and play Gaelic Football. Many of those relations, having spent most of their holidays in Ireland, have come to live in Ireland. Many of my generation who emigrated in the 50's and 60's always expressed a wish to return to Ireland to retire, but for many reasons were unable to do so. Firstly, when their families grew up they were torn between Ireland and their families. Some did return but had difficulty settling as Ireland was not the place they had left and returned again. Secondly parents had died and they had grown away from their siblings.

I was so pleased to experience the visit of the Queen of England recently. It was wonderful that she got such a great reception despite the negative vibes from some sources. I find it difficult to understand that there was such resentment considering that so many Irish people live in the UK. Without the millions of sterling that was sent over, Ireland would not be what it is today. It was always a source of amusement to me that some did not like the

English but they had no objection to receiving the sterling. Personally I have found that being Irish was a great advantage to being accepted for employment. Ireland has been repaid handsomely for any misdeeds of the past.

Without the support of my good neighbours, colleagues, friends and a very supportive partner, settling back to life in Ireland would have been much more difficult. Emigration is back on the agenda, which I think is positive as my experience has been a great learning curve. The UK has trained our nurses and many more disciplines, which people appear to forget. That trend has now reversed and nurses are trained here and then go over there. When I hear of nurses going over to the UK I just wish I was starting my career over again. I had a very interesting life and overcame many difficulties in my time. I have been respected and appreciated by many. My career has been a source of great satisfaction and given me great status in life.

I went on a nostalgia trip recently and stopped off at my family home. I looked into the overgrown garden to see the peony roses, which I planted fifty five years ago, in full bloom. I can now look at old photographs and enjoy the positive aspects of my life, which is something that I could not have done previously. My confidence and self-esteem have grown. I always felt inadequate and the black sheep of the family. This was not how colleagues, friends and relations saw me, as my life appeared to be so successful. I now see myself as the swan who was injured but has made a full recovery. I can meet up with friends from the past and enjoy reminiscing about the happy events we shared. I do appreciate the positive aspects of my life, my good health and ability to enjoy and cope with the many challenges and celebrate the good things in my life.

Epilogue

Reflecting on my life I have had many achievements in my career and in business. I also experienced much loss. My career has furnished me with psychological knowledge of the human condition and how it influences behaviour. That and the support I got from colleagues made me strong enough to overcome the difficulties which I encountered.

The only major obstacle I struggled with was personal relationships. I attribute this to the relationship between my parents during my formative years and my relationship with my mother. Her demise in 2007 has provided some closure and is strangely liberating in the sense referred to by Jeanne Safer in her book *Death Benefits*. The emotional burden I have carried all my life has disappeared. I am more confident now that I have stopped blaming myself for negative behaviour I encountered in others. Writing this book, in addition to adding to my achievements has been cathartic. It has assisted in unlocking the buried traumas of my childhood. I am very grateful to my deceased father, his example had such a positive influence on my life in so many ways. He would be enormously proud of me.

Upon reflection, I suppose the source of the family dysfunction that I experienced has to be something rooted in the society I grew up in. It was a society where our lives were planned out in advance for us; or so people thought. I learned early on not to let others make decisions for me, but this resolve invariably brought me into conflict with people around me: my family and my mother in particular.

This was also a society that had come to rely on emigration as a safety valve in many ways. It is no surprise therefore that family relations would be dysfunctional in a situation where children are being 'reared for export.' Those of our generation who went out into the world still managed to play an important role in the modernisation and development of the country. Irish people have a natural suspicion of 'foreign interference', which has meant that this contribution hasn't been altogether acknowledged or discussed. Perhaps it is time for just such a national conversation. My story is a reflection of the Irish emigrant experience and therefore a contribution to that debate.

I am fortunate in the sense that I had the opportunity to travel and work in many different countries, meeting people and seeing places which helped to broaden my horizons. But I was also able to return to the country of my birth when I was ready to do so. Some of those who left never came back. While others never had the chance to cut themselves loose.

I have no real plans for the future except to pursue my hobbies. I have peace of mind which I thought I would never achieve. I am in a positive state of mind and look forward with enthusiasm to a peaceful and happy future.